# Rethinking Armenia's Place in the Greater Middle East: Trade Dynamics, Labor Mobility, and Strategic Opportunities

*Vilen Mnatsakanyan*

Publisher: Upway Books
Author: Vilen Mnatsakanyan
Title: Rethinking Armenia's Place in the Greater Middle East: Trade Dynamics, Labor Mobility, and Strategic Opportunities
ISBN: 978-1-917916-66-0
Cover Designed on Canva: www.canva.com

contact@upwaybooks.com
www.upwaybooks.com

# Contents

# Introduction

The economic and geopolitical landscape of the Greater Middle East is undergoing profound transformation. Large-scale reforms in the member states of the Gulf Cooperation Council (GCC), the shift toward knowledge-based economies, accelerated infrastructure modernization, and the emergence of new logistical routes have turned the region into one of the most dynamically developing areas in the world. These changes create a new strategic environment in which small states — including the Republic of Armenia — gain additional opportunities to participate in regional projects and to build mutually beneficial economic partnerships. At the same time, the Middle East as a regional concept remains highly heterogeneous. Its boundaries and analytical content vary significantly across academic disciplines — international relations, economics, history, sociology — and even within individual fields. Contemporary research uses parallel terms such as Middle East, Greater Middle East, Southwest Asia and others, each of which reflects a distinct methodological approach. This makes it necessary to clarify the conceptual framework, which constitutes one of the components of this volume. Although the focus of this collection is economic, it is important to briefly note that Armenian–Arab relations have deep historical roots. Over many centuries, Armenians and the Arab world have maintained stable cultural and economic ties; at certain stages of regional history, Armenia held a particular position within the political structures of the Middle East, including during the period of the Arab Caliphate. Mentioned here only as a concise remark — without attempting a historical study — this background nonetheless provides a foundation for mutual understanding that can support contemporary economic cooperation. This volume brings together my research on Armenia's external economic relations with the Arab world, with special attention to the states of the GCC. The articles analyze the structure of Armenia's foreign trade, prospects for developing new export niches, participation in regional logistics initiatives, opportunities for exporting human capital and services, and the potential for investment cooperation. Particular emphasis is placed on the different conceptualizations of the Middle East and on how the choice of analytical frame shapes foreign economic approaches and policy decisions.

The overarching aim of these studies is to rethink Armenia's external economic strategy toward the Middle East, to outline new approaches to diversifying cooperation, strengthening long-term economic growth, and enhancing the country's economic security. As GCC states expand their global economic presence, it becomes increasingly important for Armenia to develop a strategic vision grounded in both national priorities and broader regional trends.

The research presented in this collection was carried out with the support of the Higher Education and Science Committee of the Republic of Armenia, which made it possible to approach the subject with a comprehensive and academically rigorous perspective.

# ANALYSIS OF ARMENIA'S TRADE RELATIONS WITH THE COUNTRIES OF THE GULF COOPERATION COUNCIL (GCC)

## ABSTRACT

**Relevance.** Trade relations between Armenia and the Gulf Cooperation Council (GCC) countries from the early 1990s to 2024 developed against the backdrop of the region's rapidly growing economic importance. Over the past decades, the Gulf states have assumed key positions not only in global energy, but also in trade, logistics, finance, and investment activity, transforming from a regional center into one of the important hubs of the global economy. Against this background, Armenia's trade ties with GCC countries remain limited and poorly diversified: there is a high degree of product and geographic concentration, primarily focused on the United Arab Emirates (UAE). The growth of export volumes after 2022 was driven by the expansion of a narrow range of products, while institutional fragmentation and the absence of a comprehensive foreign economic strategy continue to constrain the development of a full-fledged and sustainable partnership.

**Methods and methodology.** The study employs official statistical data on mutual trade, as well as detailed data on the commodity structure of exports and imports by trading partner and by country of origin, which made it possible to calculate the intermediary trade coefficient. Methods of structural analysis of export–import flows between Armenia and the UAE, along with retrospective and comparative approaches, provided a comprehensive understanding of the dynamics and features of trade relations.

**Results.** Statistical analysis showed a persistent concentration of trade flows on the UAE in both imports and exports. After 2022, product concentration intensified further, increasing the vulnerability of trade to external fluctuations.

**Conclusions.** The absence of an institutionalized foreign economic policy, under conditions of a short-term positive shock, reduces the likelihood of sustainable growth. Without strategic measures for diversification and strengthening of economic ties, the current trade expansion will not lead to long-term development of mutual relations.

*Keywords:* Armenia, GCC countries, foreign trade, foreign economic policy, trade structure

# INTRODUCTION

Over the past decades, the countries of the Gulf Cooperation Council (GCC) have significantly strengthened their positions in both the global and regional economy. In 1990, the share of the Gulf states in global GDP amounted to 0.84%, representing 38.16% of the total GDP of Arab countries and 27.73% of the overall GDP of the MENA region. By 2023, these figures had increased to 1.99%, 60.17%, and 48.91%, respectively (Figure 1). Alongside economic growth, the importance of GCC states as a financial, investment, and logistics hub has also increased [1]. This development is driven both by internal political stability and the implementation of national economic transformation programs, particularly the Vision 2030 strategy and similar initiatives. The active involvement of Gulf states in international trade and infrastructure projects enhances their role in the global economy and makes the region especially attractive for countries seeking to expand their foreign economic relations [2].

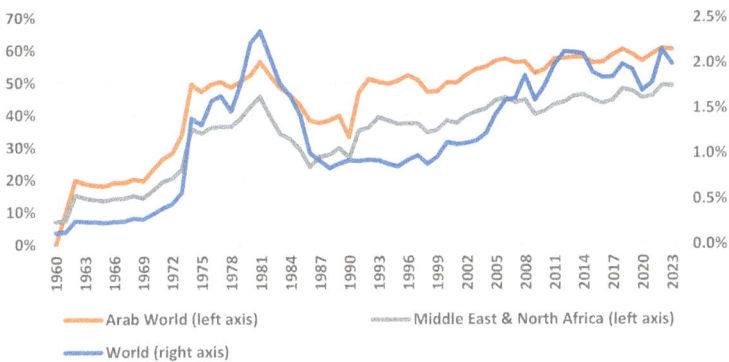

**Figure 1. Share of GCC GDP in the world, the Arab world, and the Middle East and North Africa region (%), 1960-2023.**

*Source: World Bank Database: https://data.worldbank.org/ [3]*

Given Armenia's geographical proximity to the Persian Gulf region, as well as the growing role of GCC countries in global trade, the study of the dynamics and structure of economic relations becomes particularly relevant. This is especially important in the context of increasing global turbulence and following the external economic shock of 2022, which led to the transformation of several international trade routes and the redistribution of export flows. Within this framework, a sharp increase in Armenian exports to the United Arab Emirates has been observed, while the range of exported goods remains limited [4]. From the perspective of developing Armenia's foreign trade relations with the Gulf Cooperation Council (GCC) states, particular importance lies in examining the structure of trade turnover, both in terms of exports and imports. During the period from 1995 to 2024, the United Arab Emirates (UAE) consistently occupied the position of Armenia's main export partner among the countries of the region (see Figure 2). This fact highlights the central role of the UAE in shaping Armenia's export geography toward the GCC.

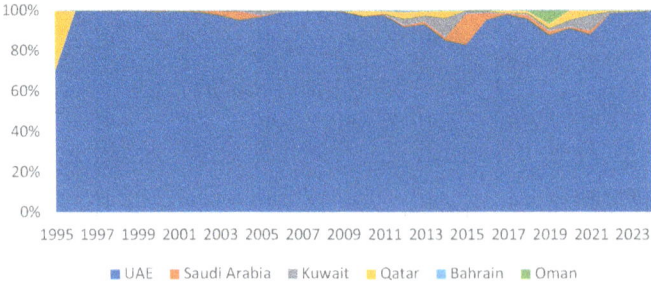

**Figure 2. Armenia's exports to GCC countries (% share by country of total exports to the GCC), 1995–2024.**

*Source: Statistical Committee of the Republic of Armenia, https://armstat.am/am/ [5]*

10

Of particular note is the growing export concentration after 2022: while in 2021 the UAE accounted for 88% of Armenia's total exports to GCC countries, by 2024 this share had reached 99.64%. Such dynamics indicate not only the increasing dependence on a single trade destination but also the absence of diversification within subregional foreign economic interaction. An analysis of Armenia's imports from the GCC demonstrates a similar picture: apart from the United Arab Emirates, the shares of other countries in Armenia's total imports from the region remain consistently low (see Figure 3). However, when imports are considered by country of origin, the structure appears less concentrated (see Figure 4), which points to the re-export nature of a significant part of the supplies. This suggests that a considerable share of goods entering Armenia from GCC states and neighboring regions transits through the UAE. In this regard, the Emirates function not only as Armenia's primary trade partner but also as a key link in intermediary trade chains, providing both logistical and commercial intermediation in Armenia's foreign economic relations.

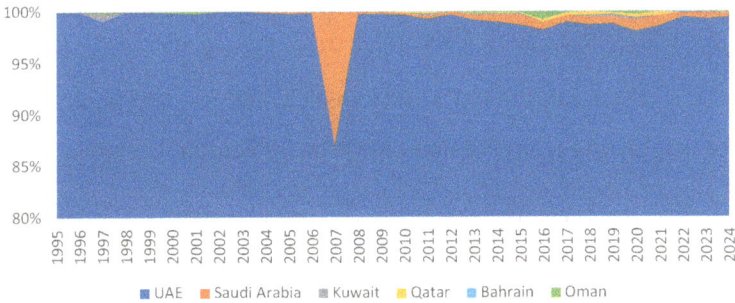

**Figure 3. Armenia's imports (by trading country) from GCC countries (% share by country of total imports from the GCC), 1995–2024.**

*Source: Statistical Committee of the Republic of Armenia, https://armstat.am/am/ [6]*

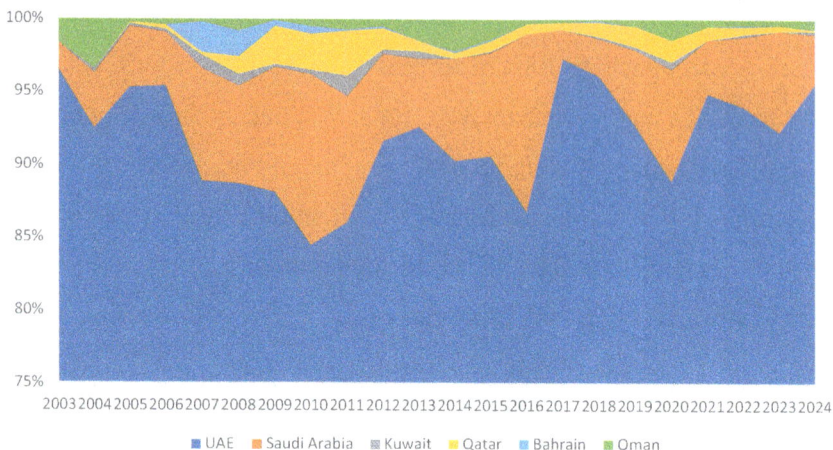

**Figure 4. Armenia's imports (by country of origin) from GCC countries (% share by country of total imports from the GCC), 2003–2024.**

*Source: Statistical Committee of the Republic of Armenia, https://armstat.am/am/ [7]*

The intermediary nature of trade flows through the UAE is further confirmed by the calculation of the intermediation trade index for the period 2003–2024. In 2024, this index reached 443%, meaning that the volume of exports from the UAE to Armenia was almost four times higher than the volume of goods produced directly within the Emirates (see Figure 5). This disproportion reflects the active use of the UAE as a logistical and re-export hub, particularly for goods originating from Asia and the broader Middle East.

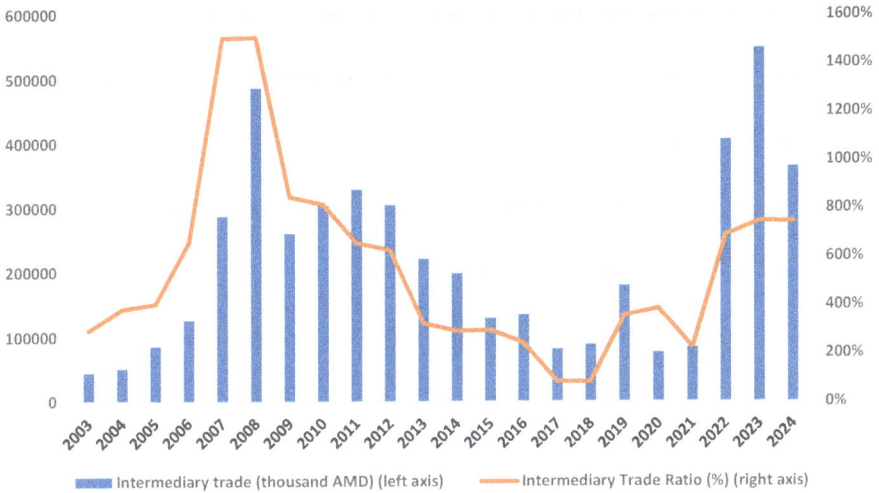

**Figure 5. Coefficient and absolute value of intermediary trade between the UAE and Armenia, 2003–2024.**

*Source: Compiled by the author based on data from the Statistical Committee of the Republic of Armenia, https://armstat.am/am/ [8]*

The intermediation trade index peaked in 2008, but in subsequent years, against the backdrop of the global financial crisis and a decline in global trade volumes, the indicator showed a downward trend. Since 2017, however, the index has been demonstrating stable growth, reflecting the increasing importance of the UAE as a logistical and intermediary trade hub in the region. Such dependence is accompanied not only by short-term trade advantages but also by the formation of strategic risks associated with one-sided geographical orientation and vulnerability to politico-economic changes in a single partner state. The findings underline the necessity of an institutional reassessment of Armenia's export-import policy with respect to Gulf countries and the transition from situational engagement to a stable and well-structured foreign economic strategy at the subregional level.

# The Economic Significance of the UAE in Armenia's Trade with the GCC

To analyze the prospects for developing Armenia's foreign economic relations with the GCC, it is essential to examine the dynamics and structure of trade with the United Arab Emirates, which in recent years has served as Armenia's key partner in this subregion. Between 2012 and 2024, trade turnover between Armenia and the UAE increased more than fortyfold in absolute terms, reaching USD 5,701,783.388 thousand. The UAE's share in Armenia's total trade turnover in 2024 stood at 18.91% (see Figure 6), with cumulative growth amounting to 244%. The main driver of this growth was exports, which provided the core momentum of bilateral trade. Thus, during the period under review, Armenia's exports to the UAE increased by approximately 5.9 times, reaching USD 13,092,206.24 thousand in 2024, which accounted for 40.14% of Armenia's total exports (see Figure 7). This figure confirms the exceptional importance of the UAE as an export destination beyond the Eurasian Economic Union (EAEU) and other traditional markets. Imports from the UAE show a less pronounced but still positive trend: since 2012, they have increased 2.5 times. In 2023, their share in Armenia's total imports was only 0.93% (see Figure 8). However, in 2024, a sharp surge occurred, with import volumes rising by 14,316%—from USD 119,213.8 thousand to USD 17,066,882.29 thousand. In relative terms, this accounted for 2.63% of Armenia's total imports.

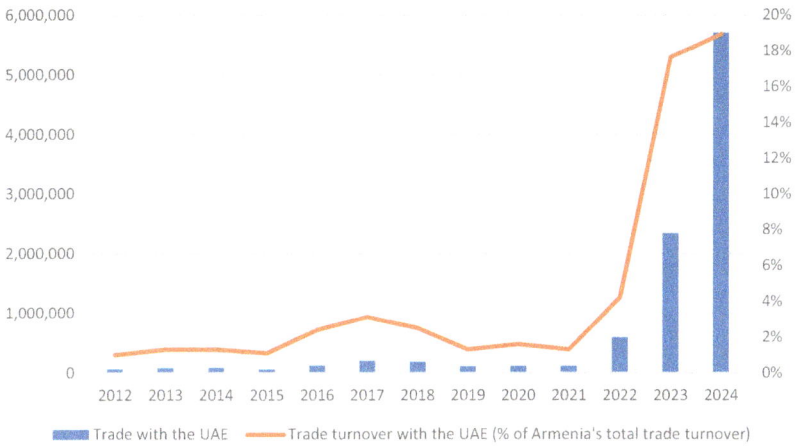

**Figure 6. Trade turnover between Armenia and the UAE (absolute value and % of total), 2012–2024.**

*Source: Statistical Committee of the Republic of Armenia, https://armstat.am/am/ [9]*

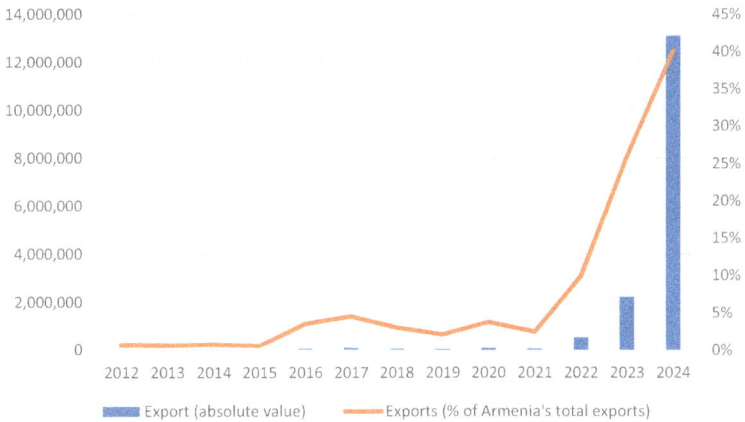

**Figure 7. Armenia's exports to the UAE (absolute value and % of total), 2012–2024.**

*Source: Statistical Committee of the Republic of Armenia, https://armstat.am/am/ [10]*

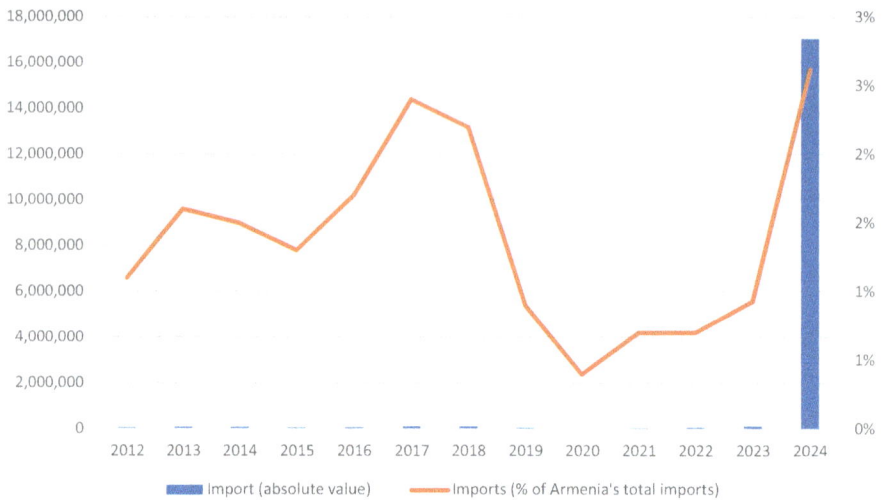

**Figure 8. Armenia's imports (by trading country) from the UAE (absolute value and % of total), 2012–2024.**

*Source: Statistical Committee of the Republic of Armenia, https://armstat.am/am/ [11]*

Therefore, the structure of bilateral trade between Armenia and the UAE is characterized by a significant predominance of exports, while the import component, despite the impressive surge in 2024, exerts a comparatively smaller influence on total trade turnover. This underscores the export-oriented nature of bilateral trade relations, as well as the high degree of asymmetry and dependence on specific trade flows. Given the scale of interaction with the UAE, the development of a sustainable foreign economic strategy for Armenia with respect to GCC countries requires a deeper analysis of institutional, logistical, and trade mechanisms, as well as an assessment of the risks associated with high concentration and limited diversification.

**Analysis of the Trade Structure between Armenia and the UAE**

An examination of the commodity structure of Armenian exports to the United Arab Emirates (UAE) in 2016–2023 reveals a persistent dependence on a limited set of product categories (see Figure 9). Moreover, the degree of concentration intensified significantly after 2022, pointing to the specific nature of export growth. During 2016–2021, the dominant category was Section 71 (precious stones, metals, and articles thereof), whose share ranged from 71.27% in 2020 to 92.16% in 2018, reflecting Armenia's critical dependence on the jewelry and gold-containing sector. Secondary export categories included machinery and equipment (Sections 84–85), articles of base metals (Sections 72–83), as well as chemical products and transport equipment (Sections 28–40 and 86–89). However, their share remained limited throughout the period. A notable change occurred in 2022, when the share of Section 71 fell to 49.94%, while Section 16–24 (food and beverages) rose to 14.02%. Other categories also expanded: Section 25–27 (mineral products) reached 2.51%, and Section 50–63 (textiles and articles thereof) accounted for 4.9%. The emergence of these directions indicates temporary diversification, most likely driven by altered logistics and transit conditions following the external economic shock of 2022. Nevertheless, by 2023 the share of Section 71 had again increased to 53.1%, confirming a return to the previous model of export dependence. At the same time, the share of Section 25–27 rose sharply to 20.94%, which may be linked to the re-export of mineral or energy resources through the UAE that were not produced in Armenia. Thus, despite temporary signs of diversification, Armenia's export structure toward the UAE remains highly concentrated, dominated by a narrow set of product categories, primarily Section 71. The increased share of Section 25–27 in 2023 only partially alters the picture, since, judging by import data, these goods most likely pass through the Emirates as a transit hub.

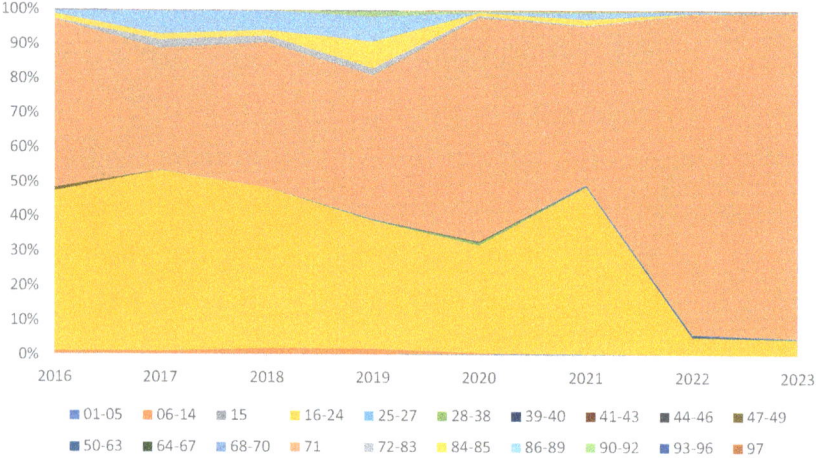

**Figure 9. Commodity structure of Armenia's exports to the UAE, 2016–2023.**

*Source: State Revenue Committee of the Republic of Armenia,* https://www.src.am/ru *[12]*

An analysis of the commodity structure of Armenia's imports from the United Arab Emirates in 2016–2023 reveals a stable concentration on a limited number of categories, making bilateral trade weakly diversified and highly vulnerable to external shocks (see Figure 10). Between 2016 and 2021, two groups dominated Armenia's imports from the UAE: Section 16–24 (foodstuffs, beverages, and tobacco) and Section 71 (precious stones, metals, and articles thereof). The share of food products ranged from 31% to 52.5%, peaking in 2017, which highlighted the role of the UAE as a mediator and logistics hub for consumer goods destined for the Armenian market. At the same time, the share of Section 71 fluctuated between 35% and 49%, demonstrating sustained demand for high-value products, often arriving via the Emirates in a re-export regime.

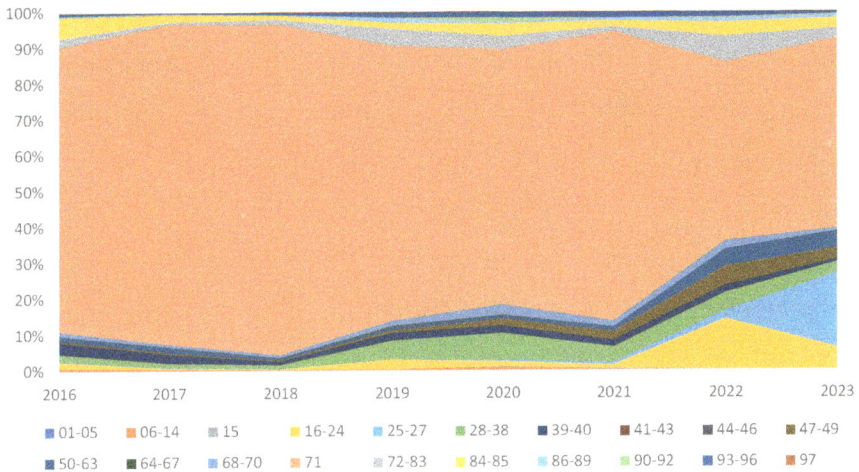

**Figure 10. Commodity structure of Armenia's imports from the UAE, 2016–2023.**

*Source: State Revenue Committee of the Republic of Armenia, https://www.src.am/ru [13]*

Against the background of relative balance in earlier years, since 2020 the import structure has shifted sharply toward the absolute dominance of Section 71. In 2020, this category accounted for 64.98% of total imports, rising to 93.4% and 94.3% in 2022 and 2023, respectively. Meanwhile, the shares of all other categories contracted dramatically: foodstuffs (Section 16–24) fell to only 5.17% in 2022 and 4.98% in 2023, while all other groups accounted for less than 1%. Thus, the structure of imports from the UAE to Armenia in recent years is characterized by a very high degree of commodity concentration, effectively reduced to imports of precious metal products. This indicates:

- the strengthening of the UAE's role as a re-export hub;
- the diminishing importance of the UAE as a universal supplier of a broad range of goods;
- the growing dependence of Armenia on a limited set of imports highly sensitive to price, geopolitical, and logistical fluctuations.

19

Unlike exports, where a short-term diversification was observed in 2022, the import structure has become even more homogeneous, which increases Armenia's vulnerability and reduces the resilience of trade relations. Furthermore, the absence of growth in industrial and technological imports (Sections 84–85, 86–89) also indicates the underdevelopment of industrial cooperation between the two countries. The analysis shows that, in shaping a long-term trade strategy toward the GCC countries, Armenia needs to:

- stimulate the expansion of the range of imported goods from the UAE;
- activate institutional and B2B platforms targeting industrial and agricultural supply chains;
- integrate imports from the UAE into strategic sectors of domestic consumption and processing, thereby reducing dependence on a narrow range of product categories.

**Conclusion**

The conducted analysis has revealed that Armenia's trade and economic relations with the member states of the Gulf Cooperation Council (GCC) are characterized by pronounced asymmetry, limited depth, and weak commodity diversification. Between 1995 and 2024, the United Arab Emirates (UAE) effectively became Armenia's only systemic partner in the region, while economic ties with other Gulf states remained fragmented, irregular, and largely episodic in nature. Following the external economic shock of 2022, a significant increase in trade volumes with the UAE was observed; however, this surge was accompanied by even greater commodity concentration. In both exports and imports, bilateral trade became dominated by Section 71 products—precious metals and articles thereof. At the same time, the UAE functions primarily as a logistical hub and re-export center rather than as a direct supplier or a final consumer market.

Such a structure of external economic relations indicates a high degree of dependence on a narrow range of goods and a single trade direction. This increases the vulnerability of Armenia's external sector, reduces its adaptability to external shocks, and limits the potential for sustainable and balanced development of trade and economic cooperation with the Gulf region in the long term.

**Recommendations**

To strengthen and expand trade and economic relations with GCC countries, a systematic approach is required, one that takes into account the specific features of each state and the potential of individual subregions. The following measures are proposed to foster diversification and broader cooperation:

- Develop and implement a targeted national strategy for deepening ties with each GCC country.
- Diversify the product range by involving non-resource sectors such as mechanical engineering, chemicals, food processing, and information technologies.
- Support export-oriented industries through insurance, marketing assistance, certification, and diplomatic backing.
- Intensify economic diplomacy by participating in trade missions and sectoral exhibitions in the Gulf states.
- Establish mechanisms for regular monitoring of trade flows to reduce dependence on re-exports and expand direct trade.

The implementation of these measures would significantly enhance the efficiency and quality of trade and economic relations, strengthening the position of national producers and exporters in GCC markets. Institutionalizing monitoring and export-support mechanisms will systematize trade flows toward the Gulf states, thereby providing a foundation for long-term planning of bilateral relations. Such an approach will ensure resilience, predictability, and a strategic orientation of Armenia's foreign trade policy.

# REFERENCES

1. *International Monetary Fund. Middle East and Central Asia Dept.* "Gulf Cooperation Council: Pursuing Visions Amid Geopolitical Turbulence: Economic Prospects and Policy Challenges for the GCC Countries", Volume 2024: Issue 066, 2024

2. Mnatsakanian V. "Economic Relations Between Armenia and the Arab Gulf States: Risks and Opportunities". Haigazian Armenological Review Volume 44/2, Haigazian University Press, Beirut, 2024, p. 301.

3. Official website of the World Bank. URL: https://data.worldbank.org/

4. Mnatsakanian V. "Analysis of the economic relations between the Gulf countries and Armenia: the role of diaspora". National Academy of Science of the Republic of Armenia, Institute of Oriental Studies, Yerevan, 2024, P. 84-85. DOI: 10.54503/978-9939-9313-4-0

5. Official website of the Statistical Committee of the Republic of Armenia. URL: https://armstat.am/en/

6. Ibid.

7. Ibid.

8. Ibid.

9. Ibid.

10. Ibid.

11. Ibid.

12. Official website of the State Revenue Committee of the Republic of Armenia. URL: https://www.src.am/en

13. Ibid.

# PERSPECTIVES OF DIVERSIFICATION OF ARMENIAN FOREIGN ECONOMIC POLICY IN CONTEXT OF ARAB WORLD

## INTRODUCTION

Armenia, as a small and open economy, has historically been dependent on external markets. Since the Middle Ages, Armenians have acted as trade intermediaries, playing an active role in the markets of the Middle East, including the Arab world. These historical ties, however, were significantly weakened during the Soviet era, when Armenia's external economic relations were primarily concentrated within the Soviet Union, particularly with Russia and other Soviet republics. The Cold War and the isolated economic policies of Soviet Armenia led to a decline in relations with the Arab world, gradually excluding them from Armenia's external economic agenda. Consequently, after gaining independence, Armenia entered the global economy without sufficiently developed or robust connections with the Middle East, particularly the Arab countries. In recent years, amid rapid geopolitical changes, regional instability, and the emergence of new economic centers globally, diversifying Armenia's external economic policy has become increasingly urgent. In this context, the Arab world, particularly the Gulf Cooperation Council (GCC) countries, represents a promising direction for promoting exports and fostering investment cooperation.

**Key words** – Armenia, Arab World, Trade Relations, Export and Import, GCC, Mashreq, Maghreb

# THE ECONOMIC ROLE AND TRADE POTENTIAL OF THE ARAB WORLD

Over the past few decades, the economic role of the Arab world within the global economy has grown significantly, driven by fluctuations in global oil prices, as well as efforts to restructure and diversify economies. This trend is evident when examining the share of Arab countries in global Gross Domestic Product (GDP). In 1965, the GDP of Arab countries accounted for only 1.34% of global GDP, but by 2023, this share had increased to 3.31%. Notably, in 1965, several Arab states had not yet gained independence, partially explaining the lower share during that period. By contrast, in 1980 and 1981, this share reached 4.26% and 4.2% (Fig 1), respectively, driven by the global oil crisis, which led to sharp increases in oil prices and significant GDP growth in oil-producing Arab countries. However, beyond numerical growth, the structure of GDP is critical. While oil extraction and exports dominated Arab economies in previous decades, recent years have seen active diversification efforts. A notable example is the Emirate of Dubai in the United Arab Emirates (UAE), where financial services, tourism, logistics, and new technologies have become key economic drivers. In this context, the share of oil rents in the GDP of Arab countries was 17.1% in 2021, significantly lower than the 57.6% recorded in 1979. The average share from 1970 to 2021 was approximately 24.7%, with a slight increase in 2021 attributed to economic measures implemented to address the consequences of the COVID-19 pandemic. Concurrently, foreign trade has shown consistent growth. In 1970, trade accounted for approximately 60% of Arab countries' GDP, rising to 91% by 2023. The peak was recorded in 2008 at 97%, driven by continuous trade growth since 1994. The subsequent decline was largely linked to the 2008–2009 global financial crisis.

**Fig. 1 Arab World's GDP (current USD) and its share in World[1]**

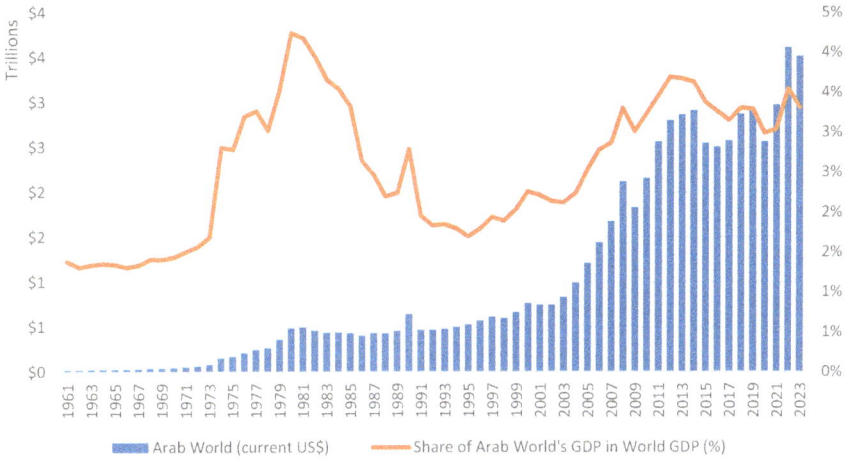

The total volume of merchandise trade in Arab countries reached USD 1.198 trillion, reflecting a 9.7% increase compared to 2022. Additionally, intra-regional trade has clear potential for growth, particularly in non-oil goods and services exports. Arab countries are increasingly exporting not only oil and petroleum products but also metals, fertilizers, precious stones, and services, particularly in transport, tourism, and finance. Thus, the Arab world's economic role continues to grow globally, but more importantly, the region is gradually shifting away from an oil-dependent model toward diversified, innovative, and service-based economies. This dynamic is particularly significant for small economies like Armenia, which can consider the Arab world as a partner not only for exports but also for investment and technological cooperation.

---

[1] Compiled by the author based on World Bank data, URL:
https://data.worldbank.org/indicator/NY.GDP.MKTP.CD

27

## CURRENT TRADE RELATIONS BETWEEN ARMENIA AND ARAB STATES

Armenia's economic relations with Arab countries are characterized by growing trade with some nations and uneven, slow development with others. From 1995 to 2023, the United Arab Emirates (UAE) has been Armenia's primary trading partner in the Arab world. Trade with the UAE has seen steady growth since the mid-2000s, particularly in recent years. In 2023, bilateral trade reached a historical peak of USD 2.846 billion, a 187.8% increase over the previous year. Since 2010, Iraq and Syria have also increased their share in Armenia's foreign trade structure, driven by regional geopolitical developments and the economic involvement of Armenian diaspora communities in these countries. However, this trend has shifted in recent years. Trade with Iraq, for instance, declined from USD 249.9 million in 2022 to USD 181.3 million in 2023, a 27.4% drop (Fig. 2), due to structural issues in Iraq's market and relatively slower growth, as well as the more rapid development of relations with the UAE. Trade relations with Syria and Lebanon, reliant on the Armenian diaspora, have been affected by prolonged socio-economic crises and military conflicts in these countries, leading to instability in trade relations despite efforts to maintain consistent ties. Egypt, while maintaining a relatively low share, demonstrates steady trade growth, reflecting gradually increasing interest and potential for long-term cooperation. Relations with other Arab countries, such as Kuwait, Oman, Qatar, Bahrain, and Morocco, remain inconsistent, with trade volumes fluctuating without sustained growth trends, indicating a lack of institutionalized foundations or stable investment and trade agendas. Overall, Armenia's trade with Arab countries is currently focused on key partners: the UAE, Iraq, Syria, Lebanon, and Egypt. The next phase of economic policy could prioritize strengthening positions in these markets while expanding ties with new markets, particularly GCC countries.

**Fig. 2 Trade turnover between Armenia and Arab states by country (% from all export to Arab states), 1995-2023[2]**

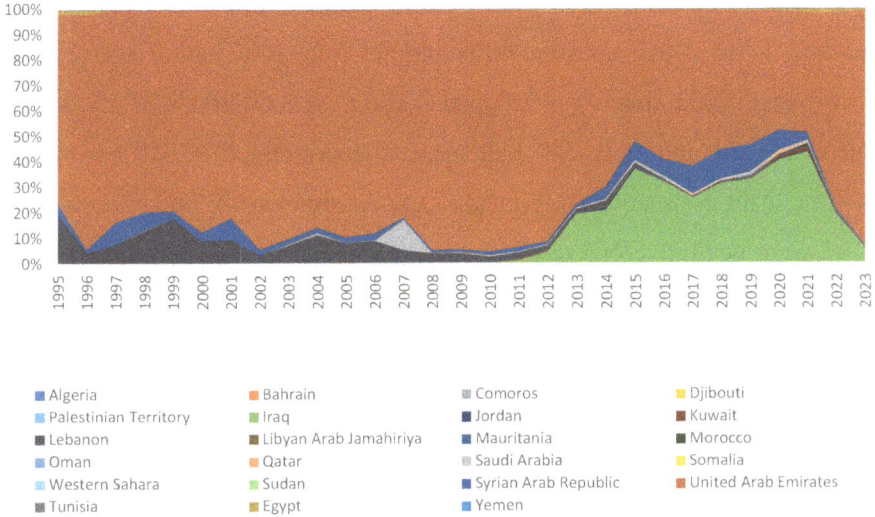

Legend:
- Algeria
- Bahrain
- Comoros
- Djibouti
- Palestinian Territory
- Iraq
- Jordan
- Kuwait
- Lebanon
- Libyan Arab Jamahiriya
- Mauritania
- Morocco
- Oman
- Qatar
- Saudi Arabia
- Somalia
- Western Sahara
- Sudan
- Syrian Arab Republic
- United Arab Emirates
- Tunisia
- Egypt
- Yemen

Armenia's export relations with Arab countries took shape in the early years of independence. In the early years of independence, the primary export destinations in the Arab world were Lebanon and Syria, driven by the presence of large, organized Armenian diaspora communities that created natural demand for Armenian goods (e.g., food products, light industry products, and beverages), historical and cultural ties, and low trade barriers in these countries. Exports to these markets were small in volume but stable, serving as Armenia's initial external markets post-independence. However, after 1995, Armenia's export structure underwent significant realignment. A new

---

[2] Compiled by the author based on data from the Statistical Service of Armenia, URL: https://armstat.am/en/

economic environment emerged in the region, driven by economic activity in parts of Iraq and the growing investment, construction, and consumer opportunities in GCC countries. Since the early 2010s, Armenia's exports have increasingly shifted toward Iraq, which became one of the leading export destinations in the Arab world for several years, driven by exports of construction materials, food products, and tobacco. In 2022, exports to Iraq reached USD 249.7 million, reflecting its role as a key export partner. However, in 2023, this figure dropped to USD 181.3 million, a 27.4% decline, due to security and logistical challenges. Concurrently, the UAE has become the dominant destination in Armenia's export structure. While exports to the UAE were negligible before 2010, they reached USD 2.84 billion in 2023, a 187.8% increase in a single year (Fig. 3), driven by the UAE's open market, investment-friendly environment, and role as a financial hub facilitating re-exports. Export relations with Egypt and other Arab countries remain limited but show modest growth trends, linked to enhanced bilateral diplomatic efforts and the introduction of new product categories. Exports to Morocco, Algeria, Tunisia, Kuwait, Oman, and Saudi Arabia remain irregular, lacking a stable partnership framework. Overall, Armenia's export structure to Arab countries has undergone a phased transformation over the past decade, shifting from diaspora-driven markets to more open, high-demand economies, serving as a critical driver for market diversification and the redefinition of Armenia's external economic strategy.

**Fig. 3 Export from Armenia to Arab states by country (% from all export to Arab states), 1995-2023[3]**

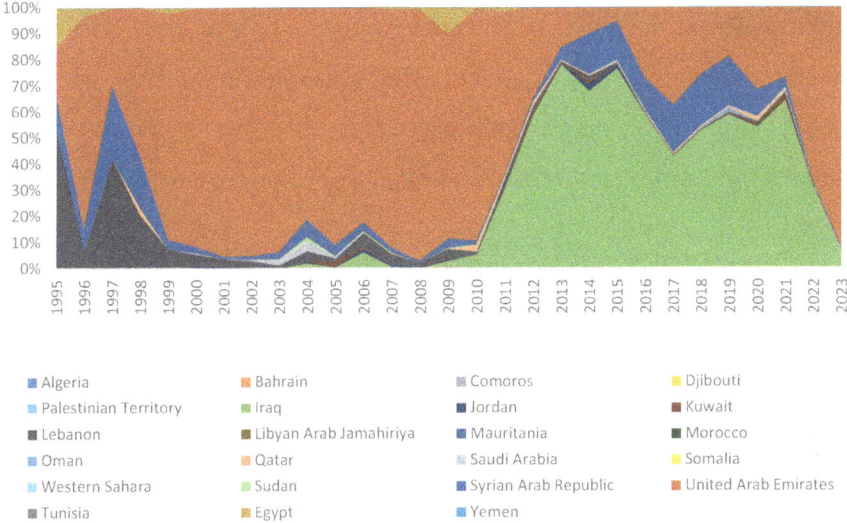

From 1995 to 2010, Armenia's import structure from Arab countries was characterized by high concentration and limited partner diversification. Analysis of bilateral import data highlights the dominant role of the United Arab Emirates (UAE). In 1995, the UAE accounted for 81.3% of imports from Arab countries, reaching up to 94.9% in 2009 in some years (Fig.4). This trend reflects Armenia's heavy reliance on a single import source, which poses risks to economic stability. Other Arab countries had significantly limited involvement in Armenia's import structure. Egypt maintained consistent but modest import shares, ranging from 0.2% to 1.8% annually. Lebanon showed some activity in the late 1990s, peaking at 18.2% in 1999, but its share declined significantly thereafter. Syria maintained low import levels (up to 3.4%) between 2000 and 2006, after which it nearly disappeared from Armenia's

[3] Compiled by the author based on data from the Statistical Service of Armenia, URL: https://armstat.am/en/

import map. Iraq's involvement began in 2001 but never exceeded 0.5% at its peak. Notably, several Arab countries, including Algeria, Bahrain, Djibouti, Comoros, Sudan, Yemen, Somalia, Western Sahara, and Libya (until 2009), were absent from import data, indicating either a lack of trade relations or negligible import volumes. These findings underscore the need for diversification of Armenia's trade partners in the Arab region to enhance economic stability and mitigate risks associated with over-reliance on a single source.

**Fig. 4 Import by country of consignment to Armenia from Arab states by country (% from all export to Arab states), 1995-2023[4]**

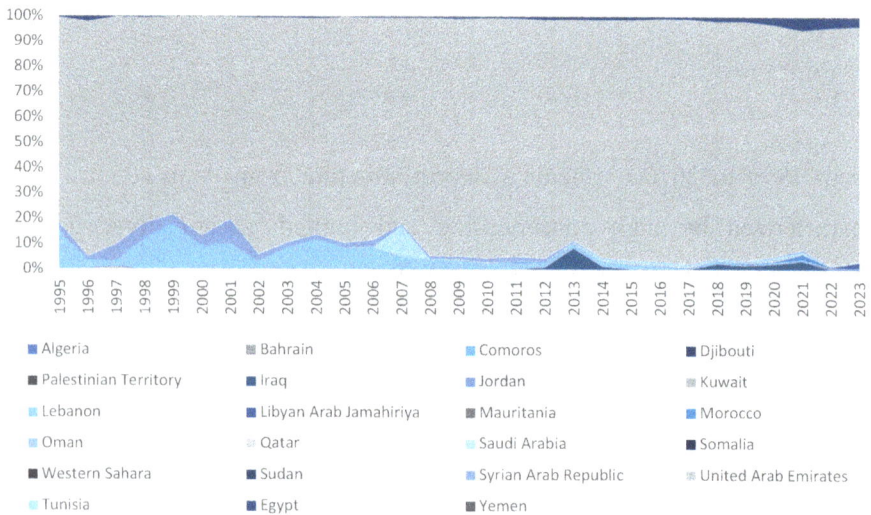

When assessing Armenia's imports from the Arab world by country of origin, a more nuanced and diversified picture emerges compared to the structure of imports based on the immediate exporting (trading) country. While the United

---

[4] Compiled by the author based on data from the Statistical Service of Armenia, URL: https://armstat.am/en/

Arab Emirates continues to dominate, its share is less overwhelming when measured by actual origin rather than by the trading intermediary. In 2023, imports originating from the UAE accounted for 54% of Armenia's total imports from Arab countries, a significant yet notably lower figure than in trade partner-based assessments. Egypt emerges as the second-largest country of origin, contributing 19.7% (Fig 5) of Arab-origin imports, followed by Libya, Morocco, Saudi Arabia, Jordan, and Tunisia, each with more modest but noteworthy shares. This distribution highlights a critical structural feature of Armenia's trade with the Arab world: a substantial portion of imports is not conducted through direct bilateral channels but rather reaches Armenia via intermediary third countries. Such a pattern suggests that formal trade relationships with many Arab states remain underdeveloped or indirect, often routed through logistics and re-export hubs such as the UAE. This reliance on intermediary trade creates inefficiencies, increases transaction costs, and limits opportunities for the establishment of stable, mutually beneficial bilateral trade frameworks. Moreover, the lack of direct import flows from a broader range of Arab countries presents a significant constraint for Armenia's foreign economic policy, as it impedes the deepening of strategic ties and the formation of long-term economic partnerships. Addressing this issue requires targeted policy interventions aimed at institutionalizing trade relations, improving logistics connectivity, and fostering diplomatic engagement to facilitate more direct commercial exchanges. By overcoming these structural barriers, Armenia could enhance the resilience, efficiency, and geopolitical balance of its trade relations with the Arab world.

**Fig. 5 Import by country of origin to Armenia from Arab states by country (% from all export to Arab states), 1995-2023[5]**

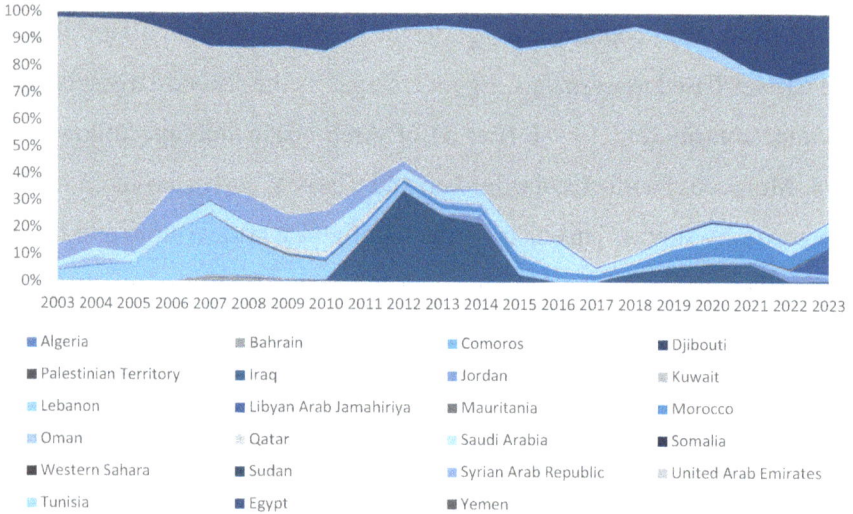

Legend:
- Algeria
- Bahrain
- Comoros
- Djibouti
- Palestinian Territory
- Iraq
- Jordan
- Kuwait
- Lebanon
- Libyan Arab Jamahiriya
- Mauritania
- Morocco
- Oman
- Qatar
- Saudi Arabia
- Somalia
- Western Sahara
- Sudan
- Syrian Arab Republic
- United Arab Emirates
- Tunisia
- Egypt
- Yemen

## Sub-Regional Approach to Economic Cooperation

In this context, it is essential to emphasize that the establishment of effective economic cooperation with the Arab world—as well as the formulation of a targeted and well-founded foreign economic policy—requires the application of a subregional approach. This approach should be based on the geographical, economic, political, and diaspora-related structural characteristics of Arab countries. From the perspective of effective analysis and policy development, four subregional groupings can be conditionally distinguished: the Mashreq (Eastern Arab countries), the Maghreb (Arab countries of Northwest Africa), the Gulf States (characterized by oil-based economies and substantial immigrant populations), and a group of other countries (e.g., Djibouti,

---

[5] Compiled by the author based on data from the Statistical Service of Armenia, URL: https://armstat.am/en/

Comoros, Mauritania) that fall outside the core strategic logic of the first three clusters. **The Mashreq region**—which includes Iraq, Syria, Lebanon, Jordan, Palestine, and Egypt—has distinctive features relevant to Armenia's foreign economic engagement. Armenia's cooperation with several countries of this group, especially Iraq and Syria, is largely shaped by the presence of a traditional Armenian diaspora and the existence of direct economic ties with the Kurdistan Region of Iraq. These connections create a specific axis of strategic partnership for Armenia. The diaspora factor is also significant for facilitating trade and investment with Lebanon and Egypt, where historically rooted Armenian communities can serve as economic and cultural bridges. **The Gulf countries (GCC)—comprising** the United Arab Emirates, Saudi Arabia, Kuwait, Qatar, Bahrain, and Oman—represent the most active and promising region for Armenia's foreign trade cooperation within the Arab world. A considerable share of Armenia's imports from Arab countries originates from the Gulf, a trend driven by several factors: the economic stability and high growth rates of these countries, the advanced development of their institutional governance systems, and their ongoing efforts toward economic diversification. It is also worth noting that a well-established Armenian diaspora exists in the Gulf, whose links with diasporic networks in Lebanon, Syria, and Egypt could further catalyze economic and investment cooperation. **The Maghreb region**—which includes Morocco, Tunisia, Algeria, Libya, and Mauritania—currently holds a lower priority on Armenia's economic agenda. However, there is growing interest in expanding trade and economic ties, particularly with Morocco and Tunisia. The potential of this subregion is of particular interest in terms of industrial cooperation and the development of linkages in the manufacturing sector. Other Arab countries outside the aforementioned subregional clusters currently occupy a marginal share in Armenia's import structure and cooperation programs. Nonetheless, under specific conditions—such as shifts in foreign policy or regional developments—some of these countries may become strategically relevant for Armenia's economic diplomacy. In conclusion, subregional classification not only allows for a more targeted formulation of Armenia's foreign economic policy toward the Arab world but also facilitates the identification of realistic pathways for deepening cooperation. These pathways are grounded in the mobilization of diaspora networks and the adaptation to existing economic and institutional realities in each subregion.

**CONCLUSION**

The analysis of Armenia's trade and economic relations with the Arab world reveals fundamental structural imbalances and a lack of strategic coherence, which hinder the realization of the full potential of these partnerships. Despite the growing importance of Arab countries in global economic and geopolitical processes, Armenia's engagement with the region remains limited, fragmented, and often reactive rather than proactive. These relations do not adequately reflect either the diverse economic opportunities presented by the Arab world or Armenia's long-term development and security interests. In this regard, the adoption of a sub-regional analytical and policy approach is not only methodologically sound but also strategically necessary. Conceptualizing the Arab world as a constellation of relatively homogeneous economic sub-zones—such as the Gulf Cooperation Council (GCC) countries, the Mashreq, the Maghreb, and other Arab states—provides a more accurate and differentiated framework for external economic policy formulation. This framework enables Armenian policymakers to take into account the significant differences across sub-regions in terms of economic structures, levels of development, institutional capacity, political stability, and the presence and influence of the Armenian diaspora. As such, it lays the groundwork for more targeted, context-sensitive, and sustainable forms of cooperation. A regionally calibrated foreign economic policy would allow Armenia to prioritize key strategic objectives such as export promotion, the diversification of trade and investment partners, technological modernization, and the attraction of foreign direct investment. Within this framework, engagement with Arab countries should not be seen in isolation but rather as a crucial component of a broader strategy to enhance Armenia's economic security and resilience. This strategic orientation would support Armenia's efforts to stabilize its position within the shifting architecture of the global economy and to more effectively respond to regional and international economic disruptions. A notable feature of Armenia's current relations with the Arab world is their heavy concentration around the GCC, and particularly the United Arab Emirates (UAE). In recent years, trade between Armenia and the UAE has grown rapidly, positioning the UAE as Armenia's dominant partner within the Arab region. However, this growth has been largely shaped by external geopolitical and economic dynamics, most notably the imposition of Western sanctions on Russia, which have led to a re-routing of trade flows and investment patterns through third-party countries, including the UAE. While this reconfiguration has created short-term opportunities for Armenia, it is also fraught with significant risks. These include over-dependence on a single partner, vulnerability to geopolitical shifts and policy changes in third countries, and exposure to regulatory uncertainty surrounding international sanctions regimes. Therefore, for Armenia to develop a stable, secure, and forward-looking economic relationship with the Arab world, it is imperative to move beyond ad hoc responses to external shocks. Instead, a comprehensive, diversified, and sub-regionally informed economic diplomacy is required—one that aligns with Armenia's broader national development strategy and supports long-term regional partnerships grounded in mutual benefit, institutional trust, and economic sustainability.

# BIBLIOGRAPHY

1. Antonyan D., "Armenia's foreign policy diversification amid new geopolitical realities", Oxford Diplomatic Society, Dispatch No. 11, page 17, 2024, URL: https://www.oxforddiplomaticsociety.com/dispatch/dispatch-no-11

2. Alrmizan M., "Armenia and Saudi Arabia: Potencial Diplomacy in Complex International Relations", King Faisal Center for Research and Islamic Studies, 2020, URL: https://kfcris.com/pdf/d3b83c3141ca90cce14914b207f5f2cc5fd7434b8afdf.pdf

3. Mnatsakanyan V., "Analysis of the economic relations between the Gulf countries and Armenia: the role of diaspora", National Academy of Sciences of the Republic of Armenia Institute of Oriental Studies, page 82, 2024, URL: https://orient.sci.am/archive/1291/article-Gz2Ylq58NkZJ9eBPFv0xXpyWfuArb47MHmDRVhgC.pdf

4. Mr. Saíd El-Naggar, "Economic Development of the Arab Countries. Selected Issues", International Monetary Fund, ISBN: 9781557753328

5. Elif Semra Ceylan and Semih Tumen, "Measuring the Economic Cost of Conflict in Afflicted Arab Countries", The Economic Research Forum, URL: https://erf.org.eg/app/uploads/2021/02/1614196316_235_439716_1459.pdf

6. IMF Report "Regional Economic Outlook. Middle East and Central Asia. An Uneven Recovery amid High Uncertainty", URL: https://www.imf.org/en/Publications/REO/MECA/Issues/2024/04/18/regional-economic-outlook-middle-east-central-asia-april-2024

7. Patricia Alonso-Gamo, Annalisa Fedelino, and Sebastian Paris Horvitz, "Globalization and Growth Prospects in Arab Countries", IMF Working Paper, 1997, URL: https://www.imf.org/external/pubs/ft/wp/wp97125.pdf

8. Xavier Sala-i-Martin and Elsa V. Artadi, "Economic Growth and Investment in the Arab World", Department of Economics, Columbia University, 2022, URL: https://core.ac.uk/download/pdf/161436734.pdf

9. Sufyan Alissa, "The Challenges of Economic Reform in the Arab World: Toward More Productive Economies", Carnegie Endowment for International Peace, 2007, URL: https://www.files.ethz.ch/isn/157936/CMEC_1_econ_reform_final.pdf

# RECONSIDERING THE CONCEPT OF THE GREATER MIDDLE EAST: PATTERNS OF REGIONAL AND SUBREGIONAL DEVELOPMENT DYNAMICS

**Abstract.** The Greater Middle East region is one of the main trend makers both in the context of geopolitical processes and in terms of geoeconomic and regional shifts in the global economic situation. Rapid economic growth and high involvement in major geopolitical processes make the study of the regional aspect of this issue extremely relevant. The purpose of this paper is to analyze the economic, demographic, and logistical aspects of the formation of this region and its current state, as well as the perception of a group of these countries as a distinct region by both external players and internal actors. The results demonstrate that by all the identified criteria, the region is extremely heterogeneous; therefore, both in terms of academic study and in the formulation of foreign policy, more attention should be paid to sub-regional processes and transformations. This can lead to the development of more effective approaches to understanding the pathways for productive engagement with the countries of the region. The main objective of this study is to analyze the existing approaches to defining the concept of the "Greater Middle East" and to reconsider its geographical boundaries in light of contemporary realities of economic interaction. This task is particularly relevant given that most regional concepts were developed within a different politico-strategic context. In the current context of geoeconomic transformations, there is a growing need to revise the region's boundaries through the lens of economic interconnectedness, trade and investment flows, and integration processes.

**Keywords:** Greater Middle East, sub-regional cooperation, geopolitics.

# 1    Introduction

The Greater Middle East region remains a hub of substantial geopolitical and economic activity, driven by its strategic energy resources, critical trade routes, and burgeoning emerging markets. Its diverse interpretations of borders underscore not only the region's geographic and cultural richness but also its pivotal economic significance. The evolving dynamics of the Greater Middle East—characterized by strong economic growth, shifting political alliances, and emerging security concerns—highlight its expanding role as a critical player in global trade and investment. By encompassing a broader region that includes the Middle East, Central Asia, and the Caucasus, this concept emphasizes the interconnectedness of economies and the potential for diversified economic relationships. The region's strategic location at the crossroads of Europe, Asia, and Africa, coupled with its wealth of energy and natural resources, positions it as a key gateway for trade and commerce. Additionally, its emerging markets offer fertile ground for investment and innovation, enabling stronger integration into the global economy. The Greater Middle East's geoeconomic role is further enhanced by its ability to serve as a bridge between major economic blocs, fostering connectivity, regional cooperation, and expanded market access. By leveraging these dynamics, the region has the potential to solidify its position as a cornerstone of international economic and geopolitical strategy.

Along with vision of the Greater Middle East, with its significant geopolitical, economic, and cultural importance, the concept of this region demands a nuanced and comprehensive understanding. While its broad characterization is widely acknowledged, a more precise definition is crucial for effective research and analysis. To fully grasp the complexities of the region, it is necessary to clearly delineate its geographical and substantive attributes, addressing key questions: What exactly defines this region? What are its boundaries? And, perhaps most importantly, what are the critical trends that shape its development?

Furthermore, exploring the Greater Middle East is not only of theoretical interest but also holds profound practical significance. In the realm of foreign policy, understanding the dynamics within and between its constituent sub-regions is essential for crafting effective strategies. This understanding can influence how countries in the region respond to external political, economic, and diplomatic signals. Equally important is recognizing whether these responses are unified across the region or whether distinct sub-regional contexts produce divergent reactions and priorities. A clear understanding of these patterns is indispensable for shaping and refining foreign policy initiatives aimed at the region.

Despite the complexity and heterogeneity of the region, the "Greater Middle East" continues to be treated as a somewhat monolithic geopolitical entity in many analytical frameworks. This paper challenges that tendency by disaggregating regional trends and identifying subregional development patterns that have emerged in response to global and domestic shifts. In doing so, it reconsiders whether the conceptualization of the Greater Middle East still holds analytical utility or whether alternative approaches may offer a more accurate representation of the region's current state and trajectory.

The objective of this research is to identify long-term patterns of economic and demographic development within the Greater Middle East, assess subregional differences, and evaluate the region's evolving role in global trade. Methodologically, the study applies a qualitative approach grounded in comparative regional analysis, supported by time series data and thematic typologies based on selected geopolitical and economic indicators. The structure of the paper proceeds as follows: Section 1 introduces the theoretical foundations and definitions related to the concept of the Greater Middle East; Section 2 outlines the key indicators used for the comparative analysis; Section 3 presents the main findings on regional and subregional dynamics; and Section 4 discusses the implications of the findings for rethinking the regional paradigm.

This paper contributes to the existing literature by offering an empirical and disaggregated perspective on a widely used but often vaguely defined concept. By linking macroeconomic patterns with geopolitical considerations, it provides new insights into how internal regional differentiation challenges established geopolitical narratives. In doing so, it adds academic value to ongoing debates on regionalism, development, and international relations in the post-globalization era.

## 2    Literature review

Defining the geographical boundaries of the Greater Middle East is a complex and multifaceted endeavor, as its delineation varies depending on the context in which it is applied. The boundaries of this region are interpreted in different ways in academic, geopolitical and cultural discourses, reflecting its diversity and complexity. However, physical boundaries are only one aspect of defining the region. Political, historical and cultural factors also play an important role, complicating the precise boundaries of the Greater Middle East. These aspects highlight the close interconnectedness of the peoples and states of the region, as well as their importance to global economics, politics and security.

The concept of the "Middle East" is historically rooted in a European perspective, which has significantly shaped Western perceptions and classifications of the region. The term was first popularized in 1902 by Alfred Thayer Mahan, an influential American naval strategist, in his article on strategic issues related to India and the Indian Ocean (Adelson, 1995). Mahan used the term to describe a geographic region of great strategic importance for shipping and trade routes, particularly to India, then a key British colony. His definition of the "Middle East" encompassed the area from the Ottoman Empire in the west to the western borders of India, including the Persian Gulf and other key areas of maritime and commercial control. This understanding of the Middle East reflects the Eurocentric view that dominated geopolitical thinking in the early 20th century. It highlights that the colonial powers viewed the region primarily through the prism of their strategic and economic interests. This perspective influenced not only how the Middle East was perceived and portrayed in Western discourse, but also the formation of its borders and political structures, especially after the collapse of the Ottoman Empire and the end of World War I.

A statistical framework commonly used to define the region is the MENA (Middle East and North Africa) classification, as reflected in World Bank studies. According to this definition, MENA encompasses 21 countries in the Middle East and North Africa (World Bank, 2024). This definition does not clearly reflect the real economic component of the region, in particular, it excludes such important countries as Turkey, Afghanistan and Pakistan, despite their obvious religious, cultural, political and economic connections with the Middle East.

In 2003, International Monetary Fund (IMF) economists Hamid Reza Davoudi and George T. Abed defined the MENA region as follows: "The MENA region includes the Arab states of the Middle East and North Africa—Algeria, Bahrain, Djibouti, Egypt, Iraq, Jordan, Kuwait, Lebanon, Libya, Mauritania, Morocco, Oman, Qatar, Saudi Arabia, Somalia, Sudan, the Syrian Arab Republic, Tunisia, the United Arab Emirates, and Yemen—as well as the Islamic State of Afghanistan, the Islamic Republic of Iran, Pakistan, the West Bank, and Gaza." The authors emphasize that the "24 MENA countries (...) are grouped together for analytical purposes only" (Abed, 2003). Despite the claim that the countries of the region "face common challenges and have cultural ties that distinguish them from neighboring economies" such as Israel and Turkey, the authors acknowledge significant religious, linguistic, and cultural diversity within the region, highlighting the presence of non-Arab nations such as Iran, Afghanistan, and Pakistan, where Arabic is not the primary language. This illustrates the limitations of the MENA framework, as it struggles to encompass the full range of political, economic, and cultural factors that shape the region. However, the definition excludes Turkey, despite its significant influence on the political, economic and military processes of the region. Turkey is actively involved in conflicts in the Middle East and is also strengthening economic ties with many MENA countries, making it an important regional player. A similar situation is observed with Israel, which, despite political differences, is an important economic and technological partner for several countries in the region.

According to the regional classification of UNAIDS (Joint United Nations Programme on HIV/AIDS), the Middle East and North Africa (MENA) region includes 19 countries. At the same time, this classification is focused on epidemiological analysis and HIV/AIDS programs, and also considers countries through the prism of common socio-economic and health challenges characteristic of the region, excluding Israel, Turkey, Iran, Afghanistan and Pakistan (UNAIDS, 2023).

Similarly, the MENA region, as defined by the United Nations High Commissioner for Refugees (UNHCR), includes 18 countries, excluding several nations that play critical roles in regional migration dynamics, such as Israel, Turkey, Iran, Afghanistan, and Pakistan (UNCHR, 2024). These countries are pivotal sources of migration and also serve as transit hubs for refugees, influencing the socio-economic and humanitarian landscape of the region. The exclusion of these countries from the UNHCR's MENA definition has been criticized, as it overlooks the significant role they play in regional migration patterns and their broader impact on regional stability.

The traditional division of the region into categories like the "Middle East" and "Near East" reflects a deeply Eurocentric perspective. From a Western cultural standpoint, such terms can be seen as an attempt to organize the world according to a framework that aligns with European geographic and strategic interests, often disregarding the internal complexity and diversity of cultures, religions, and political systems in the region. As Osman Nuri Özalp argues in his article "Where is the Middle East? The Definition and Classification Problem of the Middle East as a Regional Subsystem in International Relations", these terms are products of 19th-century Western imperialism (Özalp, 2016).

Over time, the term "Middle East" has evolved into a modern political concept that has entered international relations discourse, becoming widely adopted by the countries of the region themselves. In the post-Cold War era, and particularly after the events of September 11, 2001, new terms such as "Greater Middle East," "Broader Middle East," and "Islamic Middle East" emerged. These new definitions, especially those formulated by the United States in the context of the democratization of the Islamic world, are of particular importance for Turkey, which is considered a model country in the region.

Another alternative to the Eurocentric term "Middle East" is the designation "West Asia". This geographic term refers to the western part of Asia and is increasingly preferred in academic and analytical contexts due to its neutrality and precision. Unlike the term "Middle East," "West Asia" avoids the colonial connotations often associated with the former, offering a more geographically accurate and inclusive classification. Interestingly, the definition of "West Asia" varies depending on the context in which it is used. For instance, the United Nations Industrial Development Organization (UNIDO) includes countries such as Armenia, Georgia, and Azerbaijan in its 2015 Industrial Development Yearbook, reflecting their geographic location in the western part of Asia following the collapse of the Soviet Union (UNIDO, 2015). However, countries like Turkey and Israel, traditionally associated with the Middle East, are not included in this classification by UNIDO, likely due to their distinct political, economic, and institutional interactions with Europe and the West. This reflects a broader trend of defining regions based on industrial, economic, or geopolitical criteria, rather than purely cultural or historical factors.

In context of defining the region in framework of geopolitical and economical aspects, the prominent definition comes from Adam Garfinkle of the Foreign

Policy Research Institute, who characterizes the Greater Middle East as a region that extends beyond the traditional Middle East to include the countries of the MENA (Middle East and North Africa) region, as well as the Caucasus and Central Asia (Garfinkle, 1999). This broader definition captures a geographically expansive and interconnected area of nations that share economic, energy, and security concerns, making it a pivotal region in global economic and political discourse. This definition is significant because it highlights how economic dynamics in the region are not confined to the Middle East alone but stretch across multiple regions with growing interdependencies.

Another interpretation of the Greater Middle East in context of geopolitical dynamics emerged in the early 21st century, often associated with the "New Middle East" concept introduced by U.S. Secretary of State Condoleezza Rice in 2006 (Al Tamimi, 2013). Rice's vision of a restructured region was characterized by what she called "constructive chaos," which suggested that instability and conflict could serve as a means to realign political forces and foster democratic governance.

While this idea has been widely debated and criticized, it led to the framing of what is known as the "Great Middle East Project". This term was used to describe the U.S. and Western-led efforts to reshape the political dynamics of the region. The concept of the "New Middle East" was intended to replace the earlier and broader "Greater Middle East" term, which had been introduced by U.S. President George W. Bush in 2004, during a G-8 Summit (Wittes, 2004). The Greater Middle East under Bush's vision included not only the traditional Middle Eastern countries but also other Asian countries such as Afghanistan and Pakistan.

The "New Middle East" project, however, was marked by instability and met with skepticism as it sought to impose changes through strategic realignment and the use of chaos. As Mahdi Darius Nazemroaya of Global Research notes (Nazemroaya, 2014), the United States and Israel expected Lebanon to be a pivotal pressure point in realigning the entire region, but the result was not as planned. The geopolitical and economic consequences of this vision continue to shape regional policies today, revealing the inherent risks of pursuing instability as a means of political transformation.

Further adding to the complexity, former U.S. National Security Advisor Zbigniew Brzezinski referred to the Greater Middle East as the "Global Balkans," emphasizing its strategic significance as a critical region for Eurasia's stability and as a geopolitical focal point (Brzezinski, 1998). Brzezinski highlighted the "political awakening" in the region, suggesting that these changes signal a shift toward a multipolar world order that is reshaping the global balance of power. This evolution in the region offers new opportunities and challenges for countries like Armenia, which may need to rethink its foreign economic policy.

In conclusion, the concept of the Greater Middle East remains fluid and contested, shaped by historical, geopolitical, and cultural factors that complicate its precise definition. While frameworks like MENA and the "Greater Middle East" initiative highlight the region's strategic importance, they also reveal significant gaps in capturing its diversity, particularly regarding countries like Turkey, Israel, and Iran. Understanding these complexities is crucial for crafting effective foreign policies and addressing the region's interconnected challenges in security, economics, and diplomacy.

# 3  Methodology

This research employs a qualitative methodological approach to analyze the spatial, economic, and political dynamics of the Greater Middle East. The study is grounded in a multidimensional framework that considers geopolitical, economic, demographic, and cultural variables to examine the heterogeneity and integration patterns within the region.

The study adopts a comparative regional analysis framework, examining macroeconomic indicators and geopolitical trends across defined subregions of the Greater Middle East. The research emphasizes the necessity of a subregional lens to overcome the limitations of homogenous regional classifications such as MENA.

The data for this study were sourced from a combination of primary and secondary sources:

- **Statistical data** were extracted from reputable international databases, including:
  - The World Bank (GDP, GDP per capita, trade-to-GDP ratios, population data),
  - United Nations (UNIDO, UNAIDS, UNHCR),
  - International Monetary Fund (IMF reports on MENA),
  - National statistical agencies and regional institutions where applicable.
- **Qualitative data** were collected through an extensive literature review, including academic journals, policy reports, and strategic publications from institutions such as the Brookings Institution, the Foreign Policy Research Institute, and Global Research. This approach allowed for a comparative analysis of how the region is defined and discussed across different scholarly and policy-oriented frameworks.

The research integrates the following analytical techniques:

- **Descriptive statistical analysis** was used to assess long-term trends in GDP, GDP per capita, trade intensity, and demographic growth (1960–2023).
- **Comparative analysis** was conducted to explore inter-subregional differences in economic and demographic profiles.
- **Content analysis** of geopolitical strategies and foreign policy orientations was applied to official documents, think tank reports, and scholarly articles, capturing the strategic visions of regional actors such as Iran, Saudi Arabia, Turkey, and Israel.
- **Historical-institutional analysis** was employed to trace the evolution of regional classifications (e.g., MENA, West Asia) and their implications for geopolitical and development narratives.

## 4 Analysis/Results interpretation

### 4.1 National Self-Perception within Regional Contexts: Motivations and Stra-tegic Visions

In addition to external actors in world politics and economics, it is also important to consider the self-determination of regional players in the context of the vision of the borders of the Greater Middle East region, since it is this aspect that will allow us to better understand the motivation for the actions and strategic plans of these countries.

For Iran, the Greater Middle East is not only a geopolitical space, but also a key arena for the implementation of cultural, strategic and ideological goals. In this context, Iran seeks to strengthen its influence in countries such as Syria, Iraq, Lebanon, Yemen and the Persian Gulf, considering them as important elements of its strategy. Iran actively supports various political and armed groups, including Hezbollah, Hamas and the Houthis, not only to strengthen its regional power but also to position itself as a leader of resistance to Western interference and Israeli expansion. Iran also views Afghanistan as an important part of its geopolitical influence, especially given its ethnic and cultural ties with the Tajiks and other Shia groups, which allows it to strengthen its presence in Central Asia. Iran's influence also extends to Pakistan, where the country maintains close relations with the Shia minority and is involved in a strategic partnership with Pakistani military and political forces. Iran thus sees the region as a space where its ideological and cultural affinity with its neighboring Muslim countries allows it not only to expand its influence but also to counter strategic competitors such as the United States and Israel (Akbarzadeh, 2024).

Saudi Arabia sees the Greater Middle East as a key arena for its strategic influence and development. As part of Vision 2030, the country seeks to strengthen its position as an economic and political leader in the region by diversifying its economy, reducing its dependence on oil, and developing high-tech industries. Saudi Arabia is actively working to improve relations with neighboring countries, including Iran and Qatar, in order to stabilize the region. At the same time, it continues to maintain its traditional leadership in the Islamic world, actively participating in Arab and Muslim issues. The country also sees itself as a mediator in regional conflicts, seeking to act as a peacemaker, for example in the conflict in Yemen and the negotiations on Sudan. However, Saudi Arabia faces challenges such as the need to balance its interests with the UAE, as well as tensions with Iran, which leaves open the question of the future stability and security of the region (Jakobs, 2023).

For Turkey, the Greater Middle East is seen as a natural area of influence, which is due to the historical legacy of the Ottoman Empire. This perspective extends beyond the traditional Middle East, including the Balkans, with Turkey positioning itself as a central power capable of promoting peacemaking in the region. Recent reconciliation efforts with countries such as Syria, Egypt, the UAE, Israel, and Saudi Arabia reflect Turkey's desire to reassert its influence and stabilize the region, which is important for both its national interests and its broader geopolitical strategy. For Turkey, the Middle East remains a vital sphere of influence, and the country seeks to reassert its leadership role as it did during the Ottoman Empire. Turkey also views Pakistan as part of the region, given its strategic location vis-à-vis Iran, as well as shared security and counter-extremism interests. Turkey actively pursues ties with Pakistan, viewing it as an important partner in the context of regional security and geopolitical balances. Turkey also includes the Central Asian countries in its sphere of influence, as these states are of Turkic origin and share cultural and historical ties. Engaging with these countries, such as Kazakhstan, Uzbekistan, and Kyrgyzstan, allows Turkey to strengthen its role as an important player in the Eurasian region and develop cooperation in various areas, from economics to security (Çevik, 2024).

For Israel, the Greater Middle East is primarily defined by security issues and the changing forces in the region. Israel views the region as a place filled with existential threats, especially from Iran and its allies. The focus is on securing borders, countering Iranian expansion, and ensuring regional stability through military power and strategic alliances. Israel sees itself as an important player in reshaping the region, especially through cooperation with Sunni Arab countries such as Saudi Arabia and the UAE to counter common threats. While the Palestinian issue remains important, Israel tends to take a more gradual approach to resolving it. Ultimately, the Middle East for Israel is a region of both challenges and opportunities, where security and military alliances are critical to the country's survival and influence (Yadlin, 2024).

Thus, it can be argued that the concept of the "Greater Middle East" remains ambiguous and polysemantic, as its perception varies depending on the approaches of international organizations, academic circles, and individual regional players. In the context of international politics, for example, the United States and the European Union often view this term as an area covering the countries of the Middle East and North Africa, while countries such as Iran, Turkey, and the Arab states may interpret it in a narrower or, conversely, broader sense. This leads to the fact that there are many versions and interpretations of this concept, each of which carries historical, cultural, and political connotations. The basis for understanding this region is most often a Eurocentric concept, which is based on the geopolitical interests of the West and its ideas about the strategic importance of these territories. Such a concept to a certain extent limits the perception of the region, not taking into account, for example, the influence of Asian and Central Asian countries, as well as the role of religious and cultural ties that exist between the states of the region and its neighbors. In this study, a more extensive definition of the "Greater Middle East" will be used, which includes not only the traditional Middle East, but also the countries of North Africa, Afghanistan, Pakistan, Cyprus and Israel. This definition is based on a combination of geographical, cultural, political and religious factors, which allows for a more complete consideration of the interaction and interdependence of various actors in the region. This approach allows not only to expand the boundaries of the region, but also to identify new mechanisms and drivers of its development, which play a key role in modern geopolitical processes.

## 4.2 Economies of the countries of the Greater Middle East

The Greater Middle East has increasingly become a crucial player in the global economy. Its economic importance has grown significantly over recent decades, which is evident from its rising share of global GDP. In 1960, the region accounted for just 2.13% of the world's total GDP. By 2023, however, this share had increased to 5.5% (Figure 1), marking a substantial growth of 3.37 percentage points over the course of more than 60 years. This increase reflects the growing integration of the Greater Middle East into global economic frameworks and its expanding role in global trade, finance, and resource markets. The driving force behind this economic expansion has been primarily the region's rich natural resources, particularly oil and gas, which have historically played a dominant role in shaping its economic landscape. Oil-exporting countries within the Middle East have witnessed substantial economic growth, with revenues from energy exports fueling infrastructure development, industrialization, and diversification efforts.

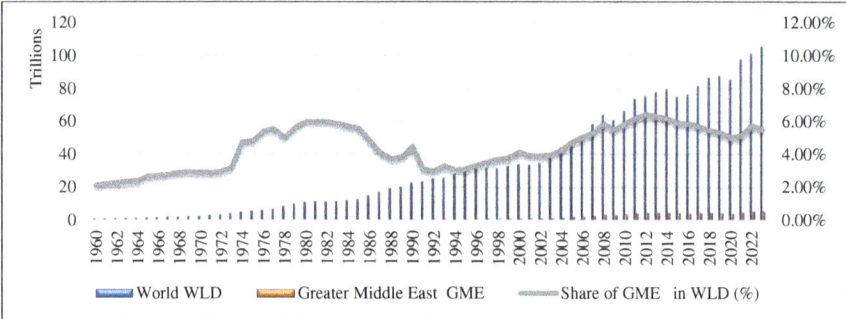

**Fig. 1.** GDP of the world and Greater Middle East countries (Trillions USD) and share of Greater Middle East countries in World GDP (%), 1960-2023

Source: *World Bank data*. The World Bank. https://data.worldbank.org/

The average economic growth of the Greater Middle East region from 1961 to 2023 has consistently outpaced the global average, reflecting the region's growing influence in the world economy (Figure 2). Over the past six decades, the region has experienced significant economic expansion, largely driven by its vast energy resources, particularly oil and natural gas. The revenue generated from oil exports has been a primary engine of growth, propelling the economies of key players like Saudi Arabia, Iran, Iraq, and others in the region. This growth has allowed the region to increase its contribution to global GDP, as discussed earlier. However, this growth trajectory is not without its challenges. The heavy reliance on oil production has created a structural vulnerability in the region's economy. While oil has been the driving force behind economic expansion, it has also made the region susceptible to fluctuations in global oil prices. The COVID-19 pandemic in 2020 exposed these vulnerabilities, as the region's economic decline was sharper than the global average. In many countries, the pandemic led to significant disruptions in trade, a slowdown in demand for oil, and a sharp drop in oil prices, all of which severely impacted the region's economic performance.

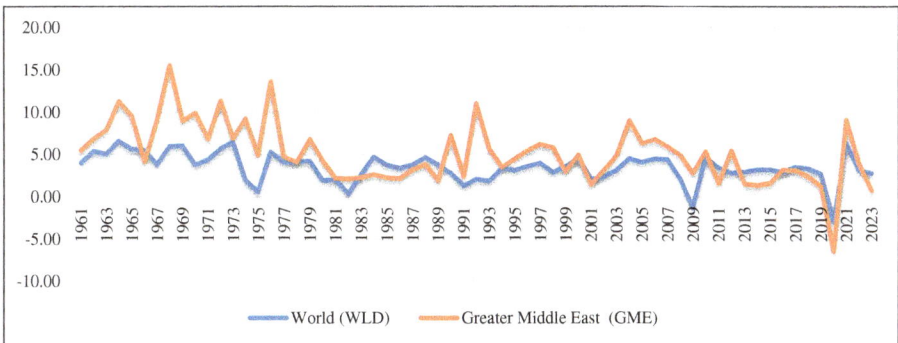

**Fig. 2.** World's and Greater Middle East countries' average economic growth (%), 1961-2023

Source: *World Bank data*. The World Bank. https://data.worldbank.org/

Despite the noticeable changes in the share of GDP of the GME countries in the world economy, it is necessary to note the different level of contribution of individual regions. One of the drivers of economic development of most countries in the region has become the raw material base (oil and gas), but the division of countries on this basis into 2 groups, oil exporters and non-exporters, is not acceptable since it does not take into account the political system, cultural, historical and religious characteristics of the countries. Therefore, it is important to analyze the total contribution of countries grouped by regions based on the stated principles.

**GCC (Gulf Cooperation Council).** The Arab Gulf countries (Saudi Arabia, UAE, Kuwait, Qatar, Oman and Bahrain) play a key role in the economy of the Greater Middle East and have a formed economic and political union in the person of the GCC. Their share in the region's GDP began to grow in the 1970s thanks to the oil boom, which allowed them to become global economic centers. The gradual diversification of their economies through infrastructure, finance, tourism and technology has allowed the Gulf countries to strengthen their positions (Hvidt, 2013). Today, they are the region's main investment donors and trade hubs, playing a leading role in global energy markets and economic development.

**Mashreq (Egypt, Syria, Jordan, Lebanon, Iraq).** The Mashreq economies, despite their historical and cultural importance, are experiencing structural difficulties (Blavy, 2001). Conflicts, political instability and a lack of reforms have led to a decline in their share of regional GDP. Iraq remains an important player due to its oil resources, but its economy is vulnerable to instability (Nawfal Kasim Ali, 2023). Egypt, the region's largest economy (N.V. Loayza, R. Odawara, 2010), has shown slow but steady growth due to investment in infrastructure and industry. Overall, the Mashreq remains a vulnerable link requiring reforms to stabilize the economy.

**Maghreb (Morocco, Algeria, Tunisia, Libya).** The Maghreb countries also have an economic and political union - the Arab Maghreb Union (AMU) and occupy a moderate position in the regional economy (IMF, 2019; ADB, 2020). Algeria and Libya rely on oil and gas exports, which makes them dependent on world energy prices (Escribano, 2016). At the same time, Morocco and Tunisia are developing agriculture, tourism and industry (M. Benabdelkader, R. Saifi, H. Saifi, 2021). Despite its potential, the Maghreb faces problems of regional integration, political instability, internal disagreements (e.g., the Western Sahara issue from the point of view of Morocco and Algeria) and economic difficulties. Reform and cooperation can make the region more competitive, using its geographical location as a bridge between Europe and the Middle East.

**Turkey.** Turkey is one of the leading economies of the Greater Middle East, occupying a stable and growing share of GDP. Its strategic location and industrial base allow it to serve as a bridge between Europe and the Middle East (D.Biro, L.Vasa, 2024). The country is actively investing in infrastructure, export-oriented industries and technology. Turkey is also increasing its geopolitical influence, which emphasizes its role as a regional leader. Turkey's economic resilience confirms its ability to maintain stable growth even in the face of external challenges (SWP Research Paper 3, 2024).

**Iran**. Iran's economic potential remains untapped due to sanctions and internal problems (Mohammad Reza Farzanegan and Esfandyar Batmanghelidj, 2023). With rich oil and gas reserves, the country could play a key role in the regional economy, but its share in the region's GDP remains stable but low. Restrictions on trade and investment are holding back growth, making the economy dependent on domestic resources. The lifting of sanctions and reforms will allow Iran to regain its position and join global markets, which will affect the economic structure of the entire region.

**Israel.** Israel has demonstrated rapid growth in economic share due to its focus on high technology and innovation (Annual Report, The State of High-Tech, 2023). Despite its small size and complex geopolitical environment, the country is a leader in scientific and technological development in the region. Innovative industries such as information technology, defense industry and agritech provide Israel with stable growth and global competitiveness. Israel serves as an example of how investment in science and knowledge can become the basis for economic success.

**Cyprus.** Cyprus plays a minor role in the regional economy due to the small size of its economy. The country focuses on tourism, shipping and financial services, taking advantage of its strategic location in the Eastern Mediterranean. However, its contribution to the GDP of the Greater Middle East remains small and stable. Cyprus maintains its role as a trade and financial hub, providing a link between Europe and the Middle East (European Commission, 2024).

**Other regions (Pakistan, Afghanistan, Sudan and Yemen).** The economies of Pakistan, Afghanistan, Sudan and Yemen have the smallest share of the region's GDP. These countries face military conflicts, political instability, poverty and weak economic bases. Pakistan, for example, has potential due to its strategic location and population size, but faces economic crises and a lack of investment (Naveed Ali, Olivier Karl Butzbach, Habib Ali Katohar and Hassan Imran Afridi, 2024). Afghanistan suffers from chronic instability and reliance on international aid (Ahmad Shekib Popal, Gurudutta P. Japee, 2024). Sudan and Yemen suffer from protracted wars and economic collapse, making them the least developed regions. These countries remain peripheral players, unable to realize their potential without significant reforms, stabilization and international support (A. Nasesr, 2023).

The economic structure of the Greater Middle East is characterized by a significant concentration of growth in the GCC countries, Turkey and Israel. At the same time, the Maghreb, Mashreq, Iran and the "other region" countries face structural development problems and political instability. Key trends include:

- The economic dominance of the GCC, secured by resource wealth and diversification.
- The successful modernization of Turkey and the innovative development of Israel.
- Iran's limited potential and the economic difficulties of the Mashreq and Maghreb.
- Marginalization of peripheral countries such as Afghanistan, Yemen and Sudan.

Another important indicator of the region's economic performance is GDP per capita. The average GDP per capita in the Greater Middle East has demonstrated a remarkable upward trajectory over the past several decades, reflecting the region's growing economic importance. In 1960, the average GDP per capita in the region was approximately 328.47 USD, while the global average stood at 450 USD. This suggests that, in the early years, the region's wealth was significantly lower than the global average. However, by 2023, the situation had dramatically changed. The region's average GDP per capita had risen to 15,546.42 USD, while the global average reached 13,138.33 USD (Figure 3).

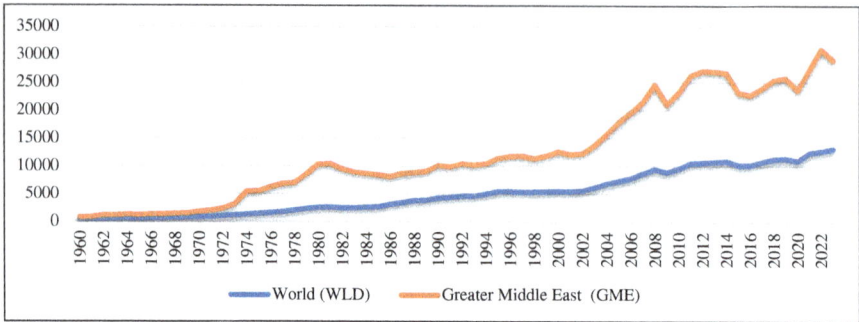

**Fig. 3.** GDP per capita (USD), average of the world and average of the Greater Mid-dle East Countries, 1960-2023

Source: *World Bank data*. The World Bank. https://data.worldbank.org/

This substantial increase of more than 15 times over the period, far outpacing the global average, highlights the significant economic growth that has occurred in the region, largely driven by the oil and gas sector. Oil wealth, alongside efforts to diversify economies into sectors such as finance, construction, tourism, and services, has propelled the region's rise in economic stature. Despite this impressive growth, it is crucial to acknowledge the disparity within the region itself. While countries like Qatar, Kuwait, and the UAE have seen their GDP per capita soar, placing them among the highest in the world, other countries in the region, especially those affected by conflict or political instability, still lag behind. For example, nations such as Yemen and Iraq continue to struggle with lower GDP per capita levels, impacted by ongoing unrest, conflict, and underdeveloped infrastructures. The increase in GDP per capita within the Greater Middle East region signifies not only the wealth generated by oil exports but also the effects of diversification efforts and modernization initiatives. However, it also points to the uneven distribution of wealth, as the region's prosperity is concentrated in a few key nations, raising important questions about the need for policies that promote broader economic growth and stability.

The presented data shows how uneven the level of economic development is in the countries of the Greater Middle East. The leader in GDP per capita in 2022 is Qatar with an impressive figure of 87,480.4 USD, which is almost 7 times higher than the world average (12,730.2 USD). This success is explained by huge revenues from oil and gas, a small population and efficient resource management. Qatar is followed by the Gulf countries such as the UAE, Kuwait, Saudi Arabia, Oman and Bahrain. Their economic position is also based on resources and active diversification of economies. Among the countries outside the GCC, Israel and Cyprus stand out. Israel shows a high level due to advanced technologies, export of knowledge-intensive products and attracting foreign investment. Cyprus, taking advantage of its status as an EU member, relies on tourism and the service sector, which helps maintain income at a fairly high level. Turkey occupies a special place. Despite the fact that its economy remains one of the largest in the region, the level of GDP per capita is still slightly below the world average. This is due to domestic economic problems: high inflation, the devaluation of the lira and an unstable political situation. However, thanks to its strong industry and advantageous geographic location, Turkey still has potential for growth. In comparison, the rest of the region lags significantly behind. The countries of North Africa - Egypt, Libya, Algeria, Tunisia and Morocco, as well as the Mashreq states, including Lebanon, Syria, Jordan and Iraq, are experiencing serious economic difficulties. The situation is even more difficult in Pakistan, Afghanistan, Yemen and Sudan, where GDP per capita figures are extremely low. The reasons are obvious: wars, political instability, weak economic diversification, high dependence on agriculture, poor infrastructure and rapid population growth. All this seriously hinders their development. Thus, a clear pattern can be seen in the grouping of countries in the region by GDP per capita. The Gulf States remain the leaders, with their success largely based on their rich natural resources and active diversification of their economies. They are joined by Israel and Cyprus, which demonstrate sustainable development thanks to technological progress and integration into global markets. Turkey occupies an intermediate position, remaining below the global average, but retaining the potential for growth due to industry and trade. At the same time, the countries of North Africa, the Mashreq, as well as Pakistan, Afghanistan and Sudan are at the opposite pole, where economic indicators remain low due to structural problems, political instability and limited resources. These differences emphasize that the economic position of the countries of the region is determined by their natural resources, political stability and successful integration into global economic processes.

## 4.3  Demographic aspect of differences within the region

Another important indicator of economic opportunity is the demographic landscape. A region's population size, growth rate, age distribution, and urbanization trends play a crucial role in shaping its economic potential. Youthful and growing populations, in particular, create opportunities for workforce expansion, innovation, and consumer market development. The demographic trajectory of the Greater Middle East over the last six decades illustrates the region's rising significance in the global context. Between 1960 and 2023, the region's share of the global population increased markedly from 6.48% to 11.48% (Figure 4). This growth underscores a profound shift in the region's demographic weight, with far-reaching economic implications. The substantial population growth presents opportunities to capitalize on an expanding consumer market, positioning the region as an attractive destination for investment in sectors such as technology, healthcare, education, and consumer goods. Urbanization accompanying this growth drives demand for infrastructure development, creating additional avenues for economic engagement. Moreover, the region's enlarging labor force provides a comparative advantage in industries requiring abundant manpower, with the potential to transition into higher-value sectors through investments in education and workforce development.

However, the demographic expansion also poses challenges. Rapid population growth necessitates increased investment in social infrastructure, including education, healthcare, and housing, to sustain equitable development. Structural issues, such as disparities in economic development across countries in the region and rising unemployment rates in certain areas, highlight the need for robust labor market policies and governance reforms. In addition to economic implications, the demographic shift enhances the region's geopolitical influence. A larger population base increases its representation and bargaining power in international forums, enabling greater participation in shaping global trade and political alliances.

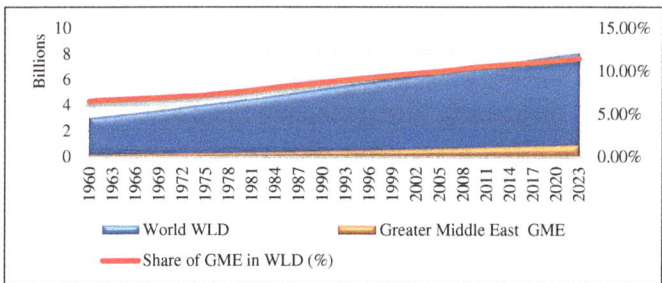

**Fig. 4.** World and the Greater Middle East countries population (billions of people) and share of GME in world population (%), 1960-2023

Source: *World Bank data*. The World Bank. https://data.worldbank.org/

The population of the Greater Middle East is distributed extremely unevenly, creating significant demographic and economic differences between countries. Several groups of countries can be distinguished by population size. Sparsely populated countries with populations of up to 5 million people include Cyprus, Mauritania, Palestine, Lebanon, as well as Kuwait, Qatar, Oman, and Bahrain. Medium-populated countries with populations of 6 to 20 million people include the UAE, Israel, Jordan, Tunisia, and Libya. Countries with populations of 21 to 50 million people include Saudi Arabia, Syria, Yemen, Morocco, Afghanistan, Iraq, Algeria, and Sudan. Large countries with populations of over 50 million people include Egypt, Turkey, Iran, and Pakistan. The share of sparsely populated countries in the total population of the region is 3.2%, medium-populated countries - 5.4%, countries with a population of 21 to 50 million people - 34.1%, and large countries - 57.3%. This distribution demonstrates significant differences in the scale of demographic potential, which directly affects the economic role of countries in the region. At the same time, the dynamics of population growth are also uneven. Some countries, such as Pakistan, Afghanistan and Egypt, demonstrate growth due to high natural increase. At the same time, the Gulf states are actively increasing their population due to the influx of migrants. The structure of migration flows in the region varies: from Pakistan, Egypt and Afghanistan, mainly low-skilled labor comes to the Gulf countries, while highly skilled specialists are sent to the same countries from Lebanon and Jordan. Refugees from Syria and Palestine most often find refuge in Turkey, which becomes a transit point on the way to the European Union. Thus, the region's population not only varies in size, but is also subject to different growth factors, which shape its economic and social dynamics.

An analysis of population density dynamics in the Middle East and North Africa since 1960 reveals significant differences between regions with high population density and areas with low population density, due to both natural-geographical and socio-economic factors. This heterogeneity is particularly noticeable when comparing countries with large but sparsely populated desert areas and states where limited territorial resources are combined with rapid demographic growth and urbanization processes. Countries with low population density, such as Saudi Arabia, Libya, Algeria and Oman, are characterized by the presence of large territories, most of which are desert or semi-desert zones, which limits the possibilities for settlement and economic activity. In these countries, the population is concentrated in certain, more favorable regions for life, such as coastal zones, oases or large cities. Nevertheless, even in conditions of relatively low density, population growth has been observed in recent decades, which in the future may increase pressure on resources and infrastructure. At the same time, countries with smaller territories and historically high population concentrations show a steady trend towards further growth in density, due to the population boom of the 20th century and active urbanization processes. Notable examples are Egypt, Lebanon, Israel and the Palestinian Territories, where population density reaches extremely high values. In Egypt, the population is traditionally concentrated in the Nile Valley and Delta, which leads to significant pressure on these areas in the context of continuing population growth. In Lebanon, high population concentrations are characteristic of urbanized regions such as Beirut and its suburbs, where migration and urbanization processes exacerbate the uneven distribution of resources. Israel and the Palestinian Territories, especially the Gaza Strip, are among the most densely populated areas in the world, which creates significant socio-economic and political challenges, aggravated by limited land resources and demographic growth. The Maghreb countries, including Tunisia and Morocco, show a similar trend: despite the presence of large unpopulated areas, population density increases significantly in coastal and economically developed areas, as a result of internal migration and rapid urban growth. This contrasts with neighboring Algeria and Libya, where large areas remain underdeveloped despite overall population growth. Of particular note are the resource-rich Gulf States, such as the UAE, Qatar, and Kuwait, where population density growth is due not only to natural growth but also to a significant influx of labor migrants against the backdrop of economic growth and urbanization. These processes are contributing to the formation of new demographic structures characterized by high population concentrations in certain urban centers. Thus, the dynamics of population density in the region since 1960 reflect profound socioeconomic and demographic transformations that intensify the contrast between densely populated and sparsely populated areas. High population density in countries with limited land resources and intensive urbanization creates significant challenges related to resource management, infrastructure development and ecological balance. In contrast, countries with low population density face the need to effectively develop their territory and create conditions for sustainable growth. These trends require a comprehensive approach to solving emerging problems and long-term planning aimed at balanced development of the region.

Migration processes play a key role in shaping the socio-economic and political landscape of the region. These processes can be divided into several types: emigration from the countries of the region, labor migration, internal migration, and the movement of refugees through transit countries. North Africa has traditionally been one of the major migrant-donor regions, with a noticeable population flow to Europe and the GCC countries. For example,

Saudi Arabia, where about a million Egyptians lived in 2020, is an important migration destination. At the same time, countries such as Egypt receive huge volumes of international remittances, which have become even more significant in the context of the COVID-19 pandemic. Labor migration remains a key aspect, especially in the GCC countries. States such as the UAE, Kuwait and Qatar, where the share of migrants in the total population is 70-80%, are significantly dependent on foreign labor in construction, services and other sectors. This creates complex migration challenges related to the protection of migrants' rights, especially in the context of these countries' increasing role on the global stage. Particular attention should be paid to internal migration processes and displacement within the region. For example, a significant number of Egyptians are resettled in other countries in North Africa and the Middle East, including internal displacement caused by socio-economic crises or climate change. For example, in the context of Palestinian migration, many displaced persons have found refuge in Egypt. Climate change also has a significant impact on migration in the region, although there are differences in the approaches of countries. Poorer states such as Libya, Algeria and Morocco face a lack of resources to adapt to climate change, which is already leading to internal displacement caused by droughts and wildfires. In contrast, GCC countries are actively investing in infrastructure and climate change adaptation projects. Such differences in approaches create an additional incentive for migration to the Gulf countries, in addition to traditional labor migration. Against this background, similar features of interaction between the countries of the region can be identified, which allows them to be divided into groups. The GCC countries play the role of the main migration centers-recipients, while North Africa, the countries of the Fertile Crescent, Afghanistan and Pakistan remain large donors of labor and refugees. Egypt, Morocco and other countries of North Africa and Turkey also play the role of transit points through which migrants and refugees move to Europe or the Gulf countries.

The demographic dynamics of the Greater Middle East play a pivotal role in shaping regional and subregional development patterns. The rapid population growth and urbanization trends present both opportunities for economic growth, such as expanding labor forces and consumer markets, and challenges, including the need for substantial investments in infrastructure and social services. Moreover, the uneven distribution of populations across the region, with varying levels of urbanization and development, underscores the complexity of addressing socio-economic disparities. Migration patterns, influenced by labor demands and geopolitical factors, further complicate the region's development dynamics, highlighting the need for nuanced policies to manage these demographic shifts and promote sustainable regional growth.

## 4.4  Trade and logistics

Another crucial indicator of economic opportunity is the trade dynamics. The patterns of imports and exports, along with trade partnerships, reflect a region's economic connectivity and growth prospects. Strong trade relations with diverse markets can open up new avenues for investment and development, while dependency on limited markets or products can expose vulnerabilities. Additionally, trade policies, logistical infrastructure, and the ability to adapt to global market trends play a vital role in determining the region's potential for economic expansion. Thus, understanding the trade landscape is essential for identifying opportunities for growth and diversification. Trade as a percentage of GDP is a crucial indicator for understanding the economic importance of a region, as it reflects the extent to which a country or region is integrated into the global economy through trade activities. In the case of the Greater Middle

East, the growing share of trade in GDP highlights the region's increasing reliance on and contribution to international trade networks. In 1970, the average trade-to-GDP ratio in the Greater Middle East stood at 48.2%, a figure already indicative of substantial trade activity. By 2022, this ratio had risen to 80.9% (Figure 5), underscoring a significant expansion in the region's trade volume relative to its economic output. This growth demonstrates not only the region's enhanced role in global trade but also its diversification into various economic sectors, including energy, manufacturing, and services.

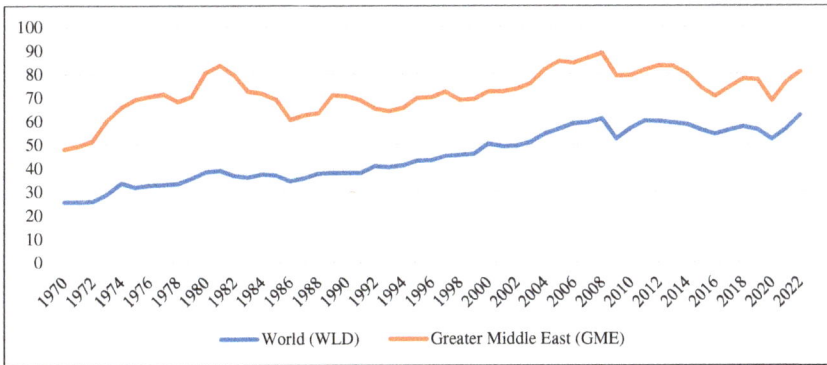

**Fig. 5.** Trade (% of GDP), average of the world and average of the Greater Middle East, 1970-2022

Source: *World Bank data*. The World Bank. https://data.worldbank.org/

Moreover, the trade-to-GDP ratio in the Greater Middle East has increased at a faster pace than the global average over the same period. This trend signifies the region's growing importance as a trade hub and its strategic position in global supply chains. Factors such as abundant natural resources, investments in infrastructure, and proactive trade agreements have contributed to this remarkable growth. The rapid development of ports, free zones, and logistical corridors has further solidified the region's status as a critical nexus for global commerce. Understanding the trade-to-GDP ratio is essential for grasping the economic dynamics of the Greater Middle East. A high and growing ratio suggests an open economy that is well-positioned to leverage globalization for economic growth. It also highlights the interdependence of the region's economies with global markets, making trade a vital component of their economic resilience and development. Consequently, the rising trade-to-GDP ratio in the Greater Middle East underscores its expanding economic influence and underscores the necessity for strategies to enhance cooperation with this pivotal region.

In context of export and import, it's important to consider also effects of logistical systems and initiatives of region. The Greater Middle East plays a key role in global logistics due to its strategic location connecting Europe, Asia and Africa. It is therefore worth noting that logistics routes are developing in both a regional and international context. Regional logistics routes include seaports, railways, pipelines and air corridors, ensuring the transportation of goods both within the region and beyond. Within the region, transport hubs are actively developing. For example, Gulf countries such as Saudi Arabia and the UAE are implementing multimodal hub projects combining seaports, airports and land routes. Oil and gas pipelines play a significant role, connecting key exporting countries such as Saudi Arabia, Kuwait and the UAE. Egypt is a key hub due to the Suez Canal, which remains one of the main routes for trade between Europe and Asia. Turkey connects Eastern Europe and the Caucasus with the Middle East, actively developing rail and road routes. The region is also integrated into global logistics chains. The Suez Canal carries up to 12% of global cargo turnover, linking the Mediterranean and Red Seas. Key routes of the Belt and Road Initiative, which connect China and Europe, pass through the countries of the region. Turkey plays an important role in the Middle Corridor, which links Central Asia and Europe. The International North-South

Transport Corridor (INSTC), which links India, Iran, Russia and Europe, is becoming increasingly important. Iran provides access to the Caspian Sea and the Persian Gulf, making it an important link in this chain. The region's logistics also depend on the migration of goods and services between the Gulf countries and South Asia. India, Oman and the UAE are actively developing sea and air corridors for the mutual exchange of products. However, the region's logistics face challenges, including political instability, military conflicts and sanctions. These factors put pressure on the sustainability of routes, but the countries of the region are actively investing in infrastructure modernization to strengthen their positions in the global logistics system. Thus, the logistics routes of the Greater Middle East provide important links both within the region and with external markets, highlighting its role as a global transport hub.

## 5    Conclusions

Based on the results of the entire analysis, it should be noted that despite the fact that the Greater Middle East region has registered high rates of economic growth both in terms of the entire economy and in terms of GDP per capita, the region's economic development is uneven: on the one hand, this is due to the issue of development sources, since a number of countries in the region have the opportunity to develop through energy exports, while others do not have such an opportunity, and on the other hand, it is also due to the structure of these economies and their foreign economic cooperation within the region. It is important to note that the GDP per capita indicator is also affected by the population level in the countries of the region, which in turn is distributed extremely unevenly: in some countries, both the population and the population density are extremely high, while in others there is a decline.

It is also important to note the perception of the region as an integral actor in foreign policy and economic processes. External players, both countries and international organizations, such as the UN and its structures, perceive the region differently, depending on the goals and visions of these players. If for UN structures the involvement of these countries in certain global processes, such as the fight against HIV or poverty, is important, then for individual world players the issue is more about plans for geopolitical influence and questions of choosing mechanisms for establishing relations with these countries.

In the context of self-perception of the countries of the Greater Middle East region as an integral region, it is also necessary to note significant differences: based on the level of development, political plans and strategies, as well as geographical location and cultural and religious aspects, countries within the region see the borders of the region differently.

Thus, it can be established that the Greater Middle East region is extremely heterogeneous in terms of the level of development, volumes and rates of population change, foreign economic relations and involvement in integration processes. In this context, studying the entire region within the framework of common metrics and methods may not give the desired result: both in the context of academic research and practical development of foreign policy, it is important to consider sub-regional processes and developments for a more effective understanding of this region.

# References

1. **Abed, G.T., Davoodi, H.R.**: Challenges of Growth and Globalization in the Middle East and North Africa. International Monetary Fund, Washington, D.C. (2003). https://www.elibrary.imf.org/display/book/9781589062290/9781589062290.xml, last accessed 2024/12/22.

2. **Adar, Sinem**: Turkey in MENA, MENA in Turkey: Reasons for Popularity, Limits to Influence, SWP Research Paper 3, Stiftung Wissenschaft und Politik (2024). https://www.swp-berlin.org/publications/products/research_papers/2024RP03_TurkeyInMENA.pdf

3. **Adelson, R.**: London and the Invention of the Middle East: Money, Power, and War, 1902–1922. Yale University Press, New Haven (1995).

4. **Ahmad Shekib Popal and Gurudutta P. Japee**: Afghanistan: From Aid Dependence to Economic Independence (2024). https://www.researchgate.net/publication/383648931_AFGHANISTAN_FROM_AID_DEPENDENCE_TO_ECONOMIC_INDEPENDENCE

5. **Akbarzadeh, S., Azizi, H.**: Iran in the Middle East: Introduction. Middle East Council (2024, April). https://mecouncil.org/publication_chapters/iran-in-the-middle-east-introduction/, last accessed 2025/01/02.

6. **Ali, Naveed; Butzbach, Olivier Karl; Katohar, Habib Ali; Afridi, Hassan Imran**: Structural and External Barriers to Pakistan's Economic Growth (2024). https://www.researchgate.net/publication/385619188_Structural_and_External_Barriers_to_Pakistan's_Economic_Growth_Pathways_to_Sustainable_Development

7. **Blavy, Rodolphe**: Trade in the Mashreq: An Empirical Examination, IMF Working Paper WP/01/163 (2001).

8. **Brzezinski, Z.**: The Grand Chessboard: American Primacy and Its Geostrategic Imperatives. Basic Books, New York (1998).

9. **Çevik, S.**: Turkey's reconciliation efforts in the Middle East: Ambitions and constraints in a changing regional order. Research Paper No. 2024RP15, German Institute for International and Security Affairs (SWP), Berlin (2024). https://www.swp-ber-lin.org/publications/products/research_papers/2024RP15_Turkey_Reconci liationMiddleEast.pdf, last accessed 2024/12/27.

10. **Escribano, Gonzalo**: The Impact of Low Oil Prices on Algeria, Columbia University Center on Global Energy Policy (2016). https://www.energypolicy.columbia.edu/sites/default/files/energy/The%20 Impact%20of%20Low%20Oil%20Prices%20on%20Algeria.pdf

11. **Farzanegan, Mohammad Reza and Batmanghelidj, Esfandyar**: Understanding Economic Sanctions on Iran: A Survey (2023). https://www.degruyterbrill.com/document/doi/10.1515/ev-2023-0014/html?lang=en

12. **Garfinkle, A.**: The Greater Middle East 2025. Foreign Policy Research Institute (1999). https://www.fpri.org/article/1999/12/the-greater-middle-east-2025/, last accessed 2025/01/03.

13. **Hvidt, Martin**: Economic Diversification in GCC Countries: Past Record and Future Trends, London School of Economics (2013). https://core.ac.uk/download/pdf/19578014.pdf

14. **International Monetary Fund (IMF)**: Economic Integration in the Maghreb: An Untapped Source of Growth, IMF Departmental Paper (2019).

15. **Israel Innovation Authority**: 2023 Annual Report: The State of High-Tech (2023). https://innovationisrael.org.il/en/report/high-techs-contribution-to-the-economy/

16. **Jakobs, A.**: Understanding Saudi Arabia's recalibrated foreign policy. International Crisis Group (2023, September). https://www.crisisgroup.org/middle-east-north-africa/gulf-and-arabian-peninsula/saudi-arabia/understanding-saudi-arabias, last accessed 2025/01/04.

17. **Kasım Ali, Nawfal**: Oil and Economic Performance in Iraq: A Blessing or a Curse! (2023). https://www.researchgate.net/publication/389210952_Oil_and_Economic_Performance_in_Iraq_A_Blessing_or_a_Curse

18. **Loayza, Norman V. and Odawara, Rei**: Infrastructure and Economic Growth in Egypt, World Bank Policy Research Working Paper No. 5177 (2010). https://www.researchgate.net/publication/46443885_Infrastructure_and_economic_growth_in_Egypt

19. **Mohamed Benabdelkader, Rachid Saifi and Hichem Saifi**: Sustainable Agriculture in Some Arab Maghreb Countries (Morocco, Algeria, Tunisia) (2021). https://www.researchgate.net/publication/355186659_Su

20. **Nazemroaya, M.D.**: Plans for redrawing the Middle East: The project for a "New Middle East". Global Research (2014, June 14). https://www.globalresearch.ca/plans-for-redrawing-the-middle-east-the-project-for-a-new-middle-east/3882, last accessed 2024/12/30.

21. **Nasesr, A.**: Sudan and Yemen: Economic Collapse and the Need for Reform (2024). https://www.mdpi.com/2673-4060/5/4/56

22. **Özalp, O.N.**: Where is the Middle East? The definition and classification problem of the Middle East as a regional subsystem in international

relations. TJP 5, 5–21 (2011).
https://www.researchgate.net/publication/299453506, last accessed 2024/12/19.

23. **Popal, Ahmad Shekib and Japee, Gurudutta P.**: Afghanistan: From Aid Dependence to Economic Independence (2024).
https://www.researchgate.net/publication/383648931_AFGHANISTAN_FROM_AID_DEPENDENCE_TO_ECONOMIC_INDEPENDENCE

24. **Shekib Popal, Ahmad and Japee, Gurudutta P.**: Afghanistan: From Aid Dependence to Economic Independence (2024). [Note: same as 23, appears duplicated]

25. **UNAIDS**: Regional Factsheet: East and North Africa (2023).
https://thepath.unaids.org/wp-content/themes/unaids2023/assets/files/regional_fs_east_north_africa.pdf, last accessed 2024/12/21.

26. **UNHCR**: Situation of Stateless Persons in the Middle East and North Africa. https://www.unhcr.org/uk/media/situation-stateless-persons-middle-east-and-north-africa-laura-van-waas, last accessed 2024/12/21.

27. **UNIDO**: Industrial Development Yearbook 2015. United Nations Industrial Development Organization, Vienna (2015).
https://books.google.am/books?id=FAKMBgAAQBAJ, last accessed 2024/12/19.

28. **Wittes, T.C.**: The new U.S. proposal for a Greater Middle East Initiative: An evaluation. Brookings Institution (2004, May 10).
https://www.brookings.edu/articles/the-new-u-s-proposal-for-a-greater-middle-east-initiative-an-evaluation/, last accessed 2025/01/05.

29. **World Bank**: The World Bank in the Middle East and North Africa: Overview, p. 20.

https://documents1.worldbank.org/curated/en/675121468756587109/pdf/multi0page.pdf, last accessed 2024/12/20.

30. **World Bank**: World Bank Data. https://data.worldbank.org/, last accessed 2024/12/20.

31. **Yadlin, A., Golov, A.**: An Israeli order in the Middle East: A chance to defeat the Iranian vision for the region—and improve on the American vision. Foreign Affairs (2024, December). https://www.foreignaffairs.com/middle-east/israeli-order-middle-east, last accessed 2025/01/06.

# THE ROLE OF FOREIGN ECONOMIC RELATIONS IN GENERATING NEW EMPLOYMENT AND EXPORTING HUMAN CAPITAL: POTENTIAL OF ARMENIA'S COOPERATION WITH THE COUNTRIES OF THE GULF COOPERATION COUNCIL (GCC)

## ANNOTATION

In the context of rapid transformations of the global labor market, special attention is drawn to the experience of the countries of the Cooperation Council for the Arab States of the Persian Gulf (GCC), which have been actively implementing economic diversification strategies over the past decades. The transition from raw material dependence to the formation of innovative, high-tech and service-oriented economies is accompanied by a steady increase in demand for highly qualified labor. Leading positions are being taken by such areas as information technology, renewable energy, fintech, medicine, education and professional services. For countries with a relatively small internal labor market, such as Armenia, these processes open up new opportunities for exporting human capital. It is important to note that the traditional understanding of foreign economic relations, which focuses mainly on trade and investment flows, requires rethinking in view of the growing importance of labor mobility. Participation in the international division of labor through the export of qualified specialists can become a significant element of Armenia's long-term economic development strategy. The aim of the study is to identify areas and mechanisms for deepening Armenia's foreign economic cooperation with the GCC countries in the field of employment and labor migration. The main tasks include analyzing the structure of the labor markets of the Gulf states, studying institutional and legal barriers to labor mobility, as well as identifying the most promising sectors for attracting Armenian specialists. The methodological basis of the work is based on a comprehensive analysis of official statistics, national economic development strategies of the GCC countries, and a comparative institutional approach. The results obtained allow us to conclude that cooperation with the Persian Gulf states can become an important direction of Armenia's foreign economic policy if effective state coordination, creation of specialized professional training programs and conclusion of intergovernmental agreements. It not only promotes employment growth and human capital development, but also integrates the country into global knowledge and service creation chains.

*Keywords*: Cooperation Council for the Arab States of the Persian Gulf (GCC), human capital, labor market, Armenia, foreign economic policy, labor mobility, employment.

INTRODUCTION

In the context of the transformation of the global labor market, human capital is becoming a key resource for development. Digitalization, automation and the transition to a knowledge economy are creating a steady demand for qualified personnel, especially in the GCC countries, where large-scale economic diversification and modernization programs are being implemented. For Armenia, as a small open economy, the export of human capital can become an important direction of the foreign economic strategy. However, the limited capacity of the domestic labor market and the outflow of qualified personnel increase the importance of finding institutionalized forms of cooperation. Cooperation with the Gulf states that need highly qualified specialists opens up prospects for the formation of controlled migration flows, which will relieve the domestic market and improve the quality of employment. The aim of the study is to identify areas and mechanisms for developing cooperation between Armenia and the GCC that contribute to the creation of new jobs and the export of labor resources.Within the framework of this goal, the following tasks are solved:

• analyze the transformation of the labor markets of the Gulf states and the emerging demand for highly qualified labor;

• consider institutional and legal barriers to labor migration and professional mobility;

• identify promising sectors for attracting Armenian specialists;

• to assess possible formats of interstate and institutional cooperation in this area.

The methodological base of the study includes an analysis of the socio-economic development strategies of the GCC countries, official statistics, regulations, as well as a comparative institutional approach that allows assessing the possibilities of adapting and integrating Armenian human capital into the region's economies.

The relevance of the study is determined by the need to develop a long-term foreign economic policy of Armenia that can not only promote the development of vocational education and employment, but also ensure the country's sustainable integration into global value chains through the export of intellectual and professional potential. In this context, cooperation with the GCC can become an important tool in addressing challenges related to social migration, while at the same time contributing to strengthening Armenia's position in the international arena.

LITERATURE REVIEW

The labor markets of the countries of the Cooperation Council for the Arab States of the Persian Gulf (GCC) are characterized by structural segmentation and a steady dependence on foreign labor. Researchers note that national cadres are mainly concentrated in the public sector, while the private sector is based on migrant resources. Researchers of X. Shaiyah and Z. Sun emphasizes that foreign workers occupy key positions in both low-skilled and high-skilled fields, and nationalization programs have limited effectiveness[6]. A survey of the Omani labor market shows the dominance of the public sector and lowinvolvement of local personnel in the private sector, despite ongoing reforms[7]. The economist M. Elsayed, analyzing the labor market of the UAE, also fixes similar problems. There is an imbalance between the high level of employment of migrants and limited opportunities for the national labor force[8]. Researchers Espinosa, Fayad and Prasad provide a broader macroeconomic perspective. In their opinion, the "rent" model of the economy hinders diversification and increases dependence on hydrocarbon exports, which directly affects the structure of the labor market[9]. In terms of demography and migration, Farguez et al. 's research on Saudi Arabia and the UAE is important. The authors show that the private sector in these countries is almost entirely provided by foreign workers, and the employment structure is formed under

---

[6] Shayah, H, Sun, Z, "Employment in the GCC Countries – Current Issues and Future Trends", Advances in Social Science, Education and Humanities Research, vol. 196, p. 412–415, 2019, URL: https://www.researchgate.net/publication/330964874_Employment_in_the_Gulf_Cooperation_Council_GCC_Countries_-_Current_Issues_and_Future_Trends

[7] Tabti, B. and Troug, H. (2025). Labor Market Dynamics in Oman. IMF Staff Discussion Note, SIP/2025/034, p. 12–15. URL: https://www.imf.org/external/pubs/ft/sip/2025/SIP034.pdf

[8] Elsayed, M. (2024). "The United Arab Emirates' labour market: An overview". LSE Middle East Centre Papers, 89, p. 33–38. URL: http://eprints.lse.ac.uk/124359/1/MEC-series-89.pdf

[9] Mr. Raphael A Espinoza, Ms. Ghada Fayad and Mr. Ananthakrishnan Prasad, "The Macroeconomics of the Arab States of the Gulf", Chapter 3, p. 65–89, Oxford University Press, 2013. URL: https://www.elibrary.imf.org/display/book/9780199683796/ch003.xml

the influence of migration flows[10]. A study conducted by the GCC Statistics Center confirms that foreigners dominate the private sector, while the public sector is mainly focused on national personnel[11]. Michael Gerb notes that economic diversification is closely linked to the labor market: dependence on the "rentier state" model preserves social and institutional barriers to transformation[12]. Similarly, Vasem Mina draws attention to structural challenges: population growth increases competition for limited public sector jobs, which increases the role of migration policy[13]. Study on labor productivity in the Gulf countries[14] It shows that migrants are more likely to occupy lower positions, which affects overall labor productivity. The work of Sah and Del Bel Air reviews the latest migration and employment reforms. The authors emphasize that despite new approaches, dependence on foreign labor remains and continues to shape the socio-economic structure of the region[15].

Thus, the literature demonstrates the sustainability of key features of the GCC labor market: the dominance of migrants in the private sector, the preservation of the roleof the public sector as the main employer for citizens, and the limited effectiveness of nationalization strategies. Despite the ongoing

---

[10] F. De-Bel-Air, "Demography, Migration and the Labour Market in Saudi Arabia", GLMM - EN - No. 5/2018, URL:
https://gulfmigration.grc.net/media/pubs/exno/GLMM_EN_2018_05.pdf
[11] GCC Statistical Centre Report, "Labour statistics in the GCC countries, Q2 2024", 2025, URL: https://gccstat.org/images/gccstat/docman/publications/labourQ2-2024.pdf
[12] Herb, Michael. Labor markets and economic diversification in the Gulf Rentiers. Georgia State University. URL: https://pomeps.org/labor-markets-and-economic-diversification-in-the-gulf-rentiers
[13] Mina, Wasseem. What is the Nature of the Employment Challenge in the GCC Countries? Gulf Research Centre. URL: https://www.grc.net/publications/working-papers
[14] A.A.Erumban and A. Al-Mejren, "Expatriate jobs and productivity: Evidence from two GCC economies", Structural Change and Economic Dynamics, volume 71, 2024, URL: https://www.sciencedirect.com/science/article/pii/S0954349X24001012
[15] Nasra M. Shah, Françoise De Bel-Air. (2021). Recent Labour and Migration Reforms and Policies in the Gulf: Impact on Economies and Societies. URL: https://gulfresearchmeeting.net/documents/63c91093baf26GRM2023GLMMWorkshop.pdf

reforms, diversification and reduction of dependence on foreign labor is slow, which poses major challenges for the region's socio-economic future.

METHODOLOGY

The study uses a comparative-analytical method that allows us to compare key characteristics and identify common patterns of labor market development in different countries, as well as identify their distinctive features. This approach is complemented by elements of content analysis, which allows for a systematic study and interpretation of strategic documents, regulations and program initiatives regulating the employment sector. At the same time, statistical data processing is used, which involves working with official employment indicators, the level of qualification of the labor force, the distribution by economic sector and the dynamics of migration flows. The study focuses on identifying structural features and trends in the transformation of labor markets both in the countries of the Cooperation Council for the Arab States of the Persian Gulf (GCC) and in Armenia. In this context, the author analyzes the impact of migration processes, which is expressed in the high dependence of the economies of the Persian Gulf countries on attracting foreign labor, and also assesses the impact of state reforms aimed at improving the employment regulation system, diversifying the economy and ensuring the stability of national labor markets.

ANALYSIS OF RESULTS

Analysis of the quantitative and qualitative dynamics of the labor force in the countries of the Cooperation Council for the Arab States of the Persian Gulf (GCC) in the period from 1990 to 2024 shows a steady increase in the labor potential of the region. According to aggregated data, the total labor force in the GCC countries increased from 5.88 million in 1990 to 32.99 million[16] in 2024 (see Graph Error! Bookmark not defined.), which is equivalent to an increase of almost 5.6 times. This trend reflects both the accelerated development of the region's economy and the steady influx of foreign labor to serve the needs of the expanding construction, infrastructure and services markets.

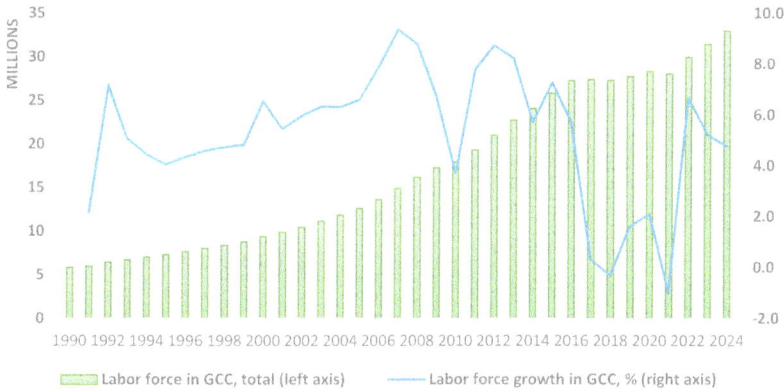

*Graph Error! Bookmark not defined.. Absolute value of the labor force in the GCC (mln people) and its growth ( % ), 1990-2024*
*Source: Compiled by the author on the World Bank database, URL: https://data.worldbank.org/*

The peak of growth was observed in the period 2005-2008, when the average annual growth was over 8%. This stage coincided with the active construction and implementation of major infrastructure projects, including in preparation for international events and strategic programs of economic modernization. In 2010-2015, a second wave of growth was observed, driven by the launch of national economic diversification programs such as Saudi Vision 2030, UAE Vision 2021, and Qatar National Vision 2030. During this period, the annual growth of the labor force averaged 6-8%. In 2020, for the first time in three decades, a decrease (-1%)[17] was recorded due to COVIDthe COVID-19 pandemic, the suspension of international mobility and a decrease in investment activity. However, by 2021, the growth rate recovered to 6.7%,

[16] World Bank's database, URL: https://data.worldbank.org/indicator/SL.TLF.TOTL.IN
[17] World Bank's database, URL: https://data.worldbank.org/indicator/SL.TLF.TOTL.IN

and in 2022-2024, it remained at the level of 4.8-5.2%[18] per year, which indicates the continuation of the structural expansion of the region's labor market. As of 2024, the total labor force in the GCC countries has reached 31.8 million people, which is 54.2%[19] of the total population of the region. Government policies in the region, including measures of the GCC Common Market and the Integrated Development Strategy, are aimed at localizing the labor force, increasing the share of citizens in high-tech and industrial sectors, overcoming structural imbalances and reducing dependence on foreign employment. The labor market retains a high external dependence and a steady demand for qualified personnel, which creates opportunities for attracting specialists from countries like Armenia who are interested in institutionalized external labor mobility.As of 2024, the countries of the Cooperation Council for the Arab States of the Persian Gulf (GCC) continue to show one of the highest proportions of migrants in the world's population structure. According to recent estimates, the largest concentration of migrant workers is recorded in Qatar (81.7 %), the United Arab Emirates (74.9%) and Kuwait (66.8%). In Saudi Arabia, migrants make up 38.7 % of the population, in Bahrain-52.8 %, and in Oman-43.2 %. On average, the share of migrants in the region reaches 59.68%[20], which confirms the stable dependence of the economies of the Persian Gulf countries on foreign labor and indicates the specific demographic structure of the region. This feature forms both socio-economic challenges and institutional features of the labor market, making the region one of the key examples of labor migration on a global scale.

The economies of the GCC countries are characterized by high diversification and technological transformation, which increases the

---

[18] Ibid
[19] Ibid
[20] Calculated by the author based on data from the World Bank and the United Nations Department of Economic and Social Affairs

importance of a highly skilled workforce. According to the WEF (2017), about 21%[21] of employees in the region belong to groups 1-3 ISCO: managers, professionals and mid-level specialists, including managers, engineers, IT specialists, scientists and doctors. The rapid development of automation and digitalization creates employment loss risks: by 2030, up to 41% of work tasks in the region can be automated, including 43-45% of functions in the UAE and Saudi Arabia[22]. In this context, there is an increasing demand for competencies in digital literacy, cybersecurity, AI, management and leadership. Retraining and advanced training programs are becoming key to maintaining the region's competitiveness in the digital economy transition.

*Saudi Arabia.* As of the first quarter of 2025, 12.8 million people were employed in the Saudi economy, of which 2.92 million were citizens of the Kingdom, and 9.88 million were non – citizens[23]. This structure of the labor market demonstrates the steady dominance of foreign labor, especially in capital-and labor-intensive industries: construction, manufacturing, administrative and support services. KSA citizens are more evenly distributed and concentrated in public services, education, healthcare, and financial and insurance activities. The main share of employment among non-citizens in Saudi Arabia (52.19% as of the first quarter of 2025) is concentrated in the unskilled category[24]. This reflects the structural advantage of the country's citizens in highly qualified segments of the labor market and confirms the existing segmentation of employment based on citizenship. Saudi citizens are concentrated in highly skilled categories (professionals, managers, clerical

---

[21] World Economic Forum, "Future of jobs and skills in the Middle East and North Africa", URL: https://www3.weforum.org/docs/WEF_EGW_FOJ_MENA.pdf
[22] Там же
[23] General Authority of Statistics of Saudi Arabia, URL: https://www.stats.gov.sa/en/statistics-tabs?tab=436312&category=124074
[24] General Authority of Statistics of Saudi Arabia, URL: https://www.stats.gov.sa/en/statistics-tabs?tab=436312&category=124074

service specialists), while non-citizens dominate in unskilled and physically intensive professions. Despite the current segmentationof the labor market, the implementation of the Vision 2030 program creates a growing demand for highly qualified labor in IT, engineering, science, renewable energy and fintech. This requires attracting foreign specialists with unique competencies through flexible migration regimes, easier recruitment, and integration into national knowledge transfer projects.

*Oman's* private sector was 86% dependent on expatriate labor in 2023[25]. The distribution of foreigners by sector shows the concentration of low-skilled labor: 17% – in construction, 13% - in agriculture, 12% - in production, 12% - in trade. The share of highly qualified employees in "other services" (including professional and technical ones) is 21%, finance and banking - 4%, tourism-3%[26]. The Omani policy of replacing foreign workers with Omanis through quotas and restrictions on hiring engineers, managers and analysts reduces the overall number of foreign specialists, but the strategic goals of Oman Vision 2040[27] to diversify the economy create niche opportunities for highly qualified experts in IT, finance and technical services.

*United Arab Emirates.* According to 2019 data, 34.2% of non-citizens have higher education (bachelor's degree-26.1%, master's degree-6.5%, doctoral degree-0.5%)[28], which ensures their dominance in highly qualified ISCO roles (groups 1-3), where they occupy 15-18% of positions in 2024. These specialists are concentrated in healthcare (3.0% of the non-citizen workforce), education (2.9%), information technology and communications

[25] Bilal Tabti and Haytem Troug, "Labor Market Dynamics in Oman", International Monetary Fund, 2025, SIP/2025/034
[26] Ibid
[27] Oman Vision 2040, URL: https://www.oman2040.om/assets/books/oman2040-en/index.html#p=33
[28] UAE Statistical Service, URL:
https://uaestat.fcsc.gov.ae/?lc=en&pg=0&snb=25&tm=labour%20force

(2.7%), finance and insurance (3.0%), as well as professional, scientific and technical activities (4.0%). Average educated non – citizens (23.1%) are employed in technical roles, such as construction (16.5%) and transport (5.7%), low-educated (25.1%) - in wholesale and retail trade (15.8%) and hotel business (4.7%)[29]. The UAE is also implementing a state program for the emiratization of the labor force[30], aimed at attracting citizens of the country to work, primarily in the private sector. This initiative, known as the Emiratiisation Policy, aims to increase the competitiveness of UAE citizens by developing professional and soft skills and ensuring their employment.From 2023, private companies with 50 or more employees are required to provide at least 2% of the employment of highly qualified specialists at the expense of UAE citizens. Starting from 2024, similar requirements apply to enterprises with a staff size of 20 to 49 people –at least one citizen, while by 2025 the quota is increased to two[31]. The mechanism of financial sanctions encourages the implementation of regulations, contributing to the transformation of the labor market, reducing dependence on foreign labor and increasing employment of citizens.

*Qatar.* In 2023, the working-age population in Qatar reached 2.5 million people, which is 2% higher than in 2022. Of this number, about 229 thousand were citizens of the country, while almost 2.3 million were foreigners (92%)[32]. Thus, every employed Qatari citizen provides for the maintenance of two members of Qatari society (in a global context, this level looks higher than the average – on average, in the world there are four employees for every ten

[29] UAE Statistical Service, URL:
https://uaestat.fcsc.gov.ae/?lc=en&pg=0&snb=25&tm=labour%20force
[30] The Government of the UAE, URL: https://u.ae/en/information-and-services/jobs/training-and-development/emiratisation
[31] Mona Elsayed, "The United Arab Emirates' labour market. An overview", LSE Middle East Centre, 2024, URL: http://eprints.lse.ac.uk/124359/1/MEC-series-89.pdf
[32] Official statistics of the Government of Qatar, URL:
https://www.data.gov.qa/pages/datastory/?stage_theme=true

employees). Among foreign workers (non – Qatari citizens), 26% are highly qualified (524,119 people), 18% are qualified (363,130 people), and 41.3% are with limited qualifications (834,654 people)[33]. Analysis of the structure of workers in Silykatar for 2023 shows that positions requiring high qualifications and related to managerial and administrative functions prevail among citizens. The most significant share is occupied by specialists (35.3%), clerks (32.55%) and managers (10.45%). This indicates a concentration of national cadres in areas that provide higher income and career opportunities. At the same time, non – citizens have the largest share in professions with low or medium qualifications: low – skilled workers make up 19.7%, artisans-16.05%, machine tool operators-8.3%. The share of specialists among them is lower (20.65%), and managers – only 1.95%[34], which indicates that senior positions are mainly concentrated in the hands of citizens. Thus, the employment structure shows a clear distribution of roles: non-citizens are mainly involved in auxiliary, service and production work, while citizens occupy most of the highly qualified and managerial positions.

Among Qatari citizens, the distribution by type of activity is more even: women predominate in highly qualified fields (45.7% are specialists), and men and women are approximately equally represented in the administrative sphere (about 32%)[35]. Non-citizens have a more polar structure: men are employed in low – skilled and technical professions, while women are employed in low-skilled service and auxiliary activities. The gender-national structure of the labor market reflects the dominance of citizens in professional and

---

[33] Ibid
[34] Official statistics of the Government of Qatar pa, URL:
https://www.data.gov.qa/pages/datastory/?stage_theme=true
[35] Official statistics of the Government of Qatar, URL:
https://www.data.gov.qa/pages/datastory/?stage_theme=true

administrative spheres and the concentration of foreign workers in less qualified positions.

Highly qualified non-citizens are one of the key drivers of modernization and innovative development of the economies of the countries of the Cooperation Council for the Arab States of the Persian Gulf (GCC). Their contribution is reflected both in the transfer of knowledge and practical experience, and in the acceleration of the introduction of advanced technologies, which is especially important in the context of the transition to a post-oil growth model. Despite the existing mechanisms of nationalization of employment and established quotas for jobs for citizens, there is a steady and largely growing demand for high-level foreign specialists. This trend is explained, on the one hand, by the predominance of low – skilled labor in the employment structure, and, on the other, by the active course of the region's countries towards economic diversification, the development of high-tech industries and the implementation of large-scale infrastructure and industrial projects. Effective policies in this area require a comprehensive approach that includes flexible and adaptive migration regimes, encouraging programs to transfer knowledge and skills to local staff, and targeted investments in education and training systems. It is important that foreign specialists not only fill the shortage of personnel, but also contribute to the formation of national human capital. It should be noted that the exclusion of Kuwait and Bahrain from this process is largely due to the limited scale of their economies and more restrained participation in international megaprojects compared to Saudi Arabia, the United Arab Emirates or Qatar. However, for most GCC countries, maintaining access to the global talent market while integrating their talent pool into national priorities is seen as one of the most important conditions for strengthening technological competitiveness, increasing productivity, and ensuring long-term sustainable economic growth.

Armenia has the potential to export human capital to the GCC countries due to the high level of education, professional training and cultural adaptability of the labor force. The growing demand for qualified specialists in the region, driven by economic diversification and digitalization, opens up opportunities for Armenian personnel in IT, healthcare, finance, engineering, education and science. The country's excess human resources are concentrated in IT, education, engineering, construction, energy, and financial services. The competitiveness of specialists is enhanced by their knowledge of foreign languages and experience in international projects. Realizing this potential requires educational and language programs, certification and professional adaptation mechanisms, as well as strategic partnerships with public and educational institutions in the Gulf countries, which will ensure sustainable migration channels and strengthen economic cooperation.At the moment, the legal framework of the Republic of Armenia contains only certain bilateral documents regulating the procedure for labor activity of Armenian citizens in certain countries of the Cooperation Council for the Arab States of the Persian Gulf (GCC). In particular, there are:

1.      Memorandum of Understanding between the Government of the Republic of Armenia and the Government of the United Arab Emirates "On Regulation of Labor Activity of Citizens of the Republic of Armenia in the United Arab Emirates"[36].

2.      Agreement between the Government of the Republic of Armenia and the Government of the State of Qatar "On Regulation of Labor Activity of Citizens of the Republic of Armenia in the Territory of the State of Qatar"[37].

---

[36] Ministry of Foreign Affairs of the Republic of Armenia, Bilateral Relations with the UAE, URL: https://www.mfa.am/en/bilateral-relations/ae
[37] Ministry of Foreign Affairs of the Republic of Armenia, Bilateral Relations with Qatar, URL: https://www.mfa.am/en/bilateral-relations/qa

The absence of legal agreements with most GCC countries restricts the protection of the rights of labor migrants from Armenia and reduces the potential for labor exports, while bilateral acts provide transparent employment conditions, social guarantees and trust in host states, creating opportunities for migration diversification.

Given the transformation of the labor market and the growing demand for qualified personnel in the GCC countries, Armenia's state employment policy is of particular importance. The Employment Development Strategy 2025-2031, approved in 2024[38], is aimed at improving the competitiveness of the labor force, reducing unemployment and adapting professional skills to the requirements of the modern market. Priorities include developing human capital, supporting young people and women, creating high-performance jobs, and introducing flexible forms of employment. The strategy creates an institutional framework for the export of labor resources, providing for retraining programs, internships, language competence development and cross-cultural adaptation of specialists in the fields of IT, engineering, finance and healthcare. It is also focused on developing youth employment centers and supporting entrepreneurship, which expands labor mobility and generates export-oriented personnel. An effective strategy requires coordination between the State, educational institutions and employers, taking into account the demand in the GCC countries. Regional cooperation opens up the potential for exporting Armenian specialists in the context of digitalization, diversification and "green" transformation of the GCC economies. Armenian cadres, as a rule, keep in touch with their homeland, which contributes to their return and strengthening the national potential. Geographical proximity facilitates professional and cultural contacts, speeding up the adaptation of the

---

[38] The RA Government Program "Strategic Employment Plan for 2025–2031 ", URL: https://www.e-gov.am/u_files/file/decrees/kar/GVAB-CCC9-B9BB-9A7C/2083.1.pdf

workforce. The main barriers to developing cooperation in the field of labor resources:

•Cultural differences – traditional values and social norms outside large metropolitan areas make it difficult to integrate foreign specialists.

•Information and transaction costs – lack of information about the labor market, difficulties with certification and participation in tenders.

•The lack of a legal framework and bilateral agreements complicates the formalization of labor relations and the systematic development of migration of highly qualified labor.

## CONCLUSIONS AND RECOMMENDATIONS

The analysis shows that Armenian human capital is characterized by a high level of education, professional training and adaptability, which makes it in demand in the GCC countries, especially in highly qualified sectors (IT, engineering, medicine, renewable energy). The economic diversification of the region creates a steady demand for such personnel, opening up opportunities for the export of labor and the parallel development of educational and labor infrastructure in Armenia.

The export of human capital from Armenia to the states of the Cooperation Council for the Arab States of the Persian Gulf (GCC) is a strategically significant area of foreign economic activity, which opens up prospects not only for increasing the level of employment within the country, but also for deepening international cooperation.

First, Armenian specialists are traditionally distinguished by a high level of education and professional training, which forms their competitive advantages in the international labor market and allows them to successfully engage in high-tech and innovative sectors of the economy.

Secondly, the Armenian labor force demonstrates the ability to adapt quickly and effectively in a multinational and multicultural environment, which is particularly important in the context of the social and ethno-cultural specifics of the GCC countries, where a significant part of the labor force consists of foreign specialists.

Third, the region's labor markets show a steady and growing demand for qualified personnel, driven by the implementation of large-scale economic diversification programs, the development of infrastructure, technological and industrial projects, as well as a focus on the formation of a post-oil growth model.

Under these conditions, Armenia, which has the appropriate human resources, is able to occupy a stable niche in providing the Persian Gulf countries with qualified specialists. Effective implementation of this potential requires a set of institutional measures, including targeted training and retraining of personnel, development of educational programs in accordance with the requirements of foreign markets, as well as systematic monitoring of employment trends in the GCC countries. This approach will not only expand the scale of labor migration, but also strengthen Armenia's position in the international labor market, ensuring the formation of stable and mutually beneficial relations. They can be based not only on the export of human capital in the traditional sense, but also on the transfer of knowledge, exchange of professional competencies and integration of Armenian specialists into key sectors of the region's economy, which will help to increase the prestige and economic significance of the country in the long term.

To realize this potential, institutional measures, targeted training of specialists and monitoring of the labor market are necessary. The export of human capital enhances Armenia's soft power, promotes knowledge transfer and strengthens international relations. In this context, it is necessary to consider the possibilities of developing bilateral relations with individual GCC countries, as well as mechanisms for creating programs at the level of the entire Union. At the same time, it is important to understand and evaluate the possibilities of creating seasonality in the export of labor services and the so-called "circular migration", in which the main economic interests of Armenian residents will remain in Armenia. Under such conditions, it is possible to achieve the results of both reducing the unemployment rate and developing mechanisms for creating added value in the production chains located in Armenia and in the GCC countries.

List of literature

1.      A.A. Erumban and A. Al-Mejren, "Expatriate jobs and productivity: Evidence from two GCC economies", Structural Change and Economic Dynamics, vol. 71, 2024, URL: https://www.sciencedirect.com/science/article/pii/S0954349X24001012

2.      Analysis of the Labor Market of the Republic of Armenia and Program Solutions for State Regulation of Employment. (2021). "Tntesaget" Publishing House; "Amberd" Research Center, in Armenian URL: https://arar.sci.am/dlibra/publication/297919/edition/273380/content

3.      Elsayed, M. (2024). The United Arab Emirates' labour market: An overview. LSE Middle East Centre Papers, 89, 33–38. URL: http://eprints.lse.ac.uk/124359/1/MEC-series-89.pdf

4.      Espinoza, Raphael A., Ghada Fayad, Ananthakrishnan Prasad. (2013). The Macroeconomics of the Arab States of the Gulf. Oxford University Press, pp. 65–89. URL: https://www.elibrary.imf.org/display/book/9780199683796/ch003.xml

5.      Fargues P., et al. (EUI/GLMM). Demography, Migration and the Labour Market in Saudi Arabia. URL: https://cadmus.eui.eu/server/api/core/bitstreams/ae5e1cf8-6592-581c-ac40-04bdf32906cb/content

6.      Fargues P., et al. (EUI/GLMM). Demography, Migration and the Labour Market in the UAE. URL: https://cadmus.eui.eu/server/api/core/bitstreams/a8eb909f-87f9-5920-b2f5-cbc647a87c41/content

7.      GCC Statistical Centre Report, "Labour statistics in the GCC countries, Q2 2024", 2025, URL: https://gccstat.org/images/gccstat/docman/publications/labourQ2-2024.pdf

8.      H. Shayah, Z. Sun, "Employment in the GCC Countries –
Current Issues and Future Trends", Advances in Social Science, Education
and Humanities Research, vol. 196, p. 412–415, 2019, URL:
https://www.researchgate.net/publication/330964874_Employment_in_the_G
ulf_Cooperation_Council_GCC_Countries_-
_Current_Issues_and_Future_Trends

9.      Herb, Michael. Labor markets and economic diversification in
the Gulf Rentiers. Georgia State University. URL: https://pomeps.org/labor-
markets-and-economic-diversification-in-the-gulf-rentiers

10.     Mina, Wasseem. What is the Nature of the Employment
Challenge in the GCC Countries? Gulf Research Centre. URL:
https://www.grc.net/publications/working-papers

11.     Nasra M. Shah, Françoise De Bel-Air. (2021). Recent Labour
and Migration Reforms and Policies in the Gulf: Impact on Economies and
Societies. URL:
https://gulfresearchmeeting.net/documents/63c91093baf26GRM2023GLMM
Workshop.pdf

12.     Oman Vision 2040. URL:
https://www.oman2040.om/assets/books/oman2040-en/index.html#p=33

13.     Program of the Government of the Republic of Armenia. (2025).
Strategic Employment Plan for 2025-2031. URL: https://www.e-
gov.am/u_files/file/decrees/kar/GVAB-CCC9-B9BB-9A7C/2083.1.pdf

14.     Randeree, K. "Workforce Nationalization in the Gulf
Cooperation Council States", CIRS, Georgetown University, 2012, URL:
https://www.files.ethz.ch/isn/141001/KasimRandereeCIRSOccasionalPaper9.
pdf

15.     S. El-Saharty, I. Kheyfets, C. H. Herbst and M. Ihsan Ajwad,
Fostering Human Capital in the Gulf Cooperation Council Countries. World

Bank Group, 2020, URL:

https://documents1.worldbank.org/curated/en/236551592799477607/pdf/Fost
ering-Human-Capital-in-the-Gulf-Cooperation-Council-Countries.pdf

16.     Tabti, B., & Troug, H. (2025). Labor Market Dynamics in Oman.
International Monetary Fund Staff Discussion Note, SIP/2025/034, 12–15.
URL: https://www.imf.org/external/pubs/ft/sip/2025/SIP034.pdf

17.     Zaidan E, "Women's labor and business participation in the
GCC: a comparative analysis of Qatar, Bahrain, and the UAE", Cogent
Social Sciences, volume 11, 2025, URL:

https://www.tandfonline.com/doi/full/10.1080/23311886.2025.2499900

18.     World Bank, Gulf Economic Update / labor & human capital
policy notes Structural Reforms and Shifting Social Norms to Increase
Women's Labor Force Participation, fall 2023, URL:

https://documents1.worldbank.org/curated/en/099145011172340921/pdf/IDU
0cb6824e50d4ed046900abd2055b4af395b3c.pdf

19.     World Economic Forum, "3 ways GCC economies are tackling
the global talent shortage", 2025.
URL:https://www.weforum.org/stories/2025/02/3-ways-gcc-economies-
tackling-the-global-talent-
shortage/#:~:text=GCC%20countries%20are%2C%20therefore%2C%20pro
moting,create%20ecosystems%20that%20cultivate%20talent.

20.     World Economic Forum, "Future of jobs and skills in the Middle
East and North Africa", 2017
URL:https://www3.weforum.org/docs/WEF_EGW_FOJ_MENA.pdf

# Conclusion

The studies presented in this collection allow us to identify the fundamental characteristics of Armenia's foreign economic engagement with the Arab world, as well as to outline areas that require strategic reconsideration. The analysis shows that despite significant growth in trade flows, especially with GCC countries, the interaction remains highly concentrated and institutionally unstable. Economic ties are predominantly focused on the United Arab Emirates, which primarily functions as a re-export and logistics hub rather than a full-fledged end market. This structure provides short-term growth but increases dependence on a single direction and heightens vulnerability to external shocks. In the broader context of the Arab world, a similar fragmentation is observed: economic activity is concentrated in a limited number of countries, while the potential for engagement with other states in the region remains largely untapped. Given the high intra-country and regional differentiation, the use of a subregional approach is justified, allowing for the consideration of the specific economic models of the Mashriq, Maghreb, GCC countries, South Caucasus, Central Asia, Horn of Africa and others. This approach improves the accuracy of the analysis and provides a basis for forming a differentiated, realistic, and long-term foreign economic strategy. The research results emphasize the need to shift from reactive, situational engagement to a strategic model focused on diversification, institutionalization, and the development of sustainable economic ties. Changes in international trade since 2022 have temporarily expanded Armenia's foreign trade opportunities; however, structural constraints — narrow product range, geographic concentration, and weak institutional mechanisms — continue to define the limits of growth. In this context, the analysis of Armenia's human capital takes on particular significance. The study shows that Armenian human capital is characterized by a high level of education, professional training, and adaptability, making it in demand in GCC labor markets, especially in highly skilled sectors such as information technology, engineering, medicine, and renewable energy. The economic diversification of the region generates steady demand for these competencies, creating opportunities not only for labor export but also for the parallel development of educational and professional infrastructure within Armenia itself.

The export of human capital to the Gulf countries represents a strategically significant direction of Armenia's foreign economic activity. Firstly, Armenian specialists possess competitive professional skills that allow them to occupy positions in sectors related to technological and innovative development. Secondly, Armenian labor demonstrates a strong ability to integrate into multicultural environments, which is particularly important given the labor market characteristics of the GCC countries, where a significant share of the workforce consists of foreign professionals. Thirdly, the implementation of large-scale diversification and industrialization programs in the Gulf states creates a stable and growing demand for qualified personnel, offering Armenia additional structural opportunities. Effective utilization of this potential requires the establishment of institutional mechanisms: programs for training and retraining personnel in accordance with GCC labor market requirements; synchronization of educational standards; development of professional certification infrastructure; and systematic monitoring of labor market changes in the region. Such an approach allows not only the creation of classical labor export flows but also conditions for circular migration, whereby the primary economic interests of specialists remain in Armenia. This provides the basis for simultaneously reducing unemployment, increasing workforce qualifications, and creating additional channels for knowledge transfer. In this context, the export of human capital can strengthen Armenia's "soft power," foster institutional interaction, deepen cooperation in key sectors, and form long-term mutually beneficial partnerships. At the bilateral level, it is advisable to develop specialized agreements with individual GCC countries, and at the multilateral level, to consider the creation of programs and mechanisms for engagement across the entire Union. This would integrate Armenian specialists into structurally significant sectors of Gulf economies while ensuring value creation within supply chains both in the GCC region and within Armenia.

Overall, the conclusions of this collection indicate that the Arab world — and especially the Gulf states — represents an important area for rethinking Armenia's foreign economic strategy. Realizing opportunities related to both trade and human capital requires a comprehensive, institutionally structured, and subregionally oriented approach. Such an approach will strengthen the country's economic resilience, increase its integration into regional processes, and create conditions for long-term economic growth and Armenia's economic security.

www.ingramcontent.com/pod-product-compliance
Lightning Source LLC
Chambersburg PA
CBHW071056280326
41928CB00050B/2525